Samuel Jones Tilden

The New York City

Samuel Jones Tilden

The New York City

ISBN/EAN: 9783337415587

Printed in Europe, USA, Canada, Australia, Japan

Cover: Foto ©Andreas Hilbeck / pixelio.de

More available books at **www.hansebooks.com**

THE

NEW YORK CITY "RING:"

ITS

ORIGIN, MATURITY AND FALL,

DISCUSSED.

THE
NEW YORK CITY "RING:"
ITS
ORIGIN, MATURITY AND FALL.

To the Times—

If one were to attempt to correct every ordinary error concerning himself which appears in print, the occasions of controversy would be inconveniently frequent for the avocations of a busy life. It is, therefore, only in a very exceptional case that I should depart from my habit of leaving such errors to answer themselves, or to be refuted by my acts, or by the general tenor of my life. But articles in the *Times* for several weeks past, so falsify the history of the events they discuss, by perverting some facts and suppressing others, that it is a right, and perhaps a duty, to vindicate the truth.

I begin by saying, that I am, in no manner or degree, responsible for this controversy. I have been concerned in no attempt to appropriate to myself, or to any set of men, or to any party, the merit of having overthrown the "Ring."

As credit with the public was no part of my motives, but only a sense of duty, founded on the idea that every personal power is a trust, I have felt no sacrifice in awarding the most liberal honors of the victory to others.

The Committee of the Bar Association will remember that, when they came to Albany with their memorial, the winning policy I indicated, was to do the work, bear the burdens, and bestow on others the honors. That policy, and the persistent forcing of the issue, in the glare of a vehement public opinion, stimulated by the nearly united Metropolitan press, did much to carry impeachment by four votes to one, over corruptions and combinations, in a body which the *Times* has characterized as venal, and in which nearly every reform failed.

Even after the work was completed, and the Bar Association met to distribute honors, I stood among its members, not to take any share to myself, but to join in a well-merited tribute of thanks to Messrs. Van Cott, Parsons and Stickney. I believe those gentlemen would avow that there was no time before the final vote in the Assembly, when, without my individual co-operation, they would have hoped for success, which needed to be organized anew, after every reverse.

Nor is it true that I was at all disposed to withhold credit from the *Times* for its services in the conflict. Its statement that Mr. Hewitt's "civil word" was the first it had received from any Democrat, is disproved by my printed speeches; and when the project—afterwards abandoned for the best motives—was entertained of offering it a public testimonial, I was applied to by its friends to join, and assented.

INSPIRATION OF ATTACKS ON ME.

What is the inspiration of its attacks upon me during the last month, I was too much out of contact with all sources of information in current politics to be able to ascertain. Could it be that its watchful rivals had discovered a morbid spot on which they delighted to put their fingers—had found they had only to mention with commendation a co-worker of the fight, in order to provoke a column of detraction? I waited. At last came an article ascribing to me a plan to control Mayor Havemeyer; characterising me as "one of the most active intriguers of the day," as attempting, "by underhand devices, to cheat the Republicans out of the fruit of their victory;" and ascribing to me "laborious stratagems,"—"wonderful mines and countermines." It asserted of me, "He has now hatched another magnificent device, and very likely supposes that the Mayor will lend himself to it." It then added, "the Legislature will do nothing of the kind." And it concluded— "If a party victory is to be claimed, *we claim it in behalf of the Republican party.*"

Next, comes a proposed charter, containing most of the worst features of the present, denying Mayor Havemeyer all substantial power over the workings of the City Government, of which he is the nominal head; putting him under guardians in the exercise of the scanty authority doled out to him; and vesting most of the governmental power and the real influence in executive offices with long terms, practically appointed by bill at Albany.

MAYOR HAVEMEYER.

Then appears another column full of similar allegations respecting me, and of what purport to be statements of facts. Among them is this: "He is said to have great influence over Mayor Havemeyer *and to be working hard to drag the Mayor into his great 'reconstruction' schemes.* Do we owe it to his influence, that the Mayor voted for Charles Shaw, as Counsel to the Board of Health?"

Now, in the whole of this mass of statement, so far as it relates to me, there is not a single atom of truth. I have not seen Mr. Havemeyer since December; nor at any time since his election, except when I met him on the street; or he called on me to ask my opinion on some question. I have not recommended or suggested to him any human being for an office, or any benefit within his gift. I do not mean to intimate that there would have been anything improper in doing so; but simply to state the fact as it is. I have not sought to influence Mr. Havemeyer in anything whatsoever. If my opinion would have any weight with him, or, on any occasion would be asked by him, it is because in almost thirty years of mutual knowledge he has looked into my mind and heart, and in no instance has seen anything which was not frank, true, disinterested and patriotic. He knows that if I had the power, which I do not pretend to have, I would not deflect him one hair's breadth from the line of fidelity to his peculiar trust, as a non-partizan representative of municipal reform, for the advantage of any party, clique or man. If he had occasion to seek my aid or counsel, he would begin by apologizing for troubling me,—so well does he know that my thoughts and tastes turn to other objects, when inclination is not overcome by a sense of duty. As to Mr. Charles P. Shaw, I do not believe I should know that gentleman if I were to meet him; and I never heard his name mentioned in connection with any appointment until I read of his being voted for as Counsel to the Board of Health, by Mr. Havemeyer.

The *Times* not only assumes to state, with absolute positiveness, my pleas and thoughts, but, also, my arguments to Republicans, and my whispers to my friends. There is not one word of truth in all these statements. I have not had any plans of reconstructing the Democratic party of the city, by any aid of patronage from Mayor Havemeyer. I do desire that the organization of the Democratic party, and of all parties, should be in the hands of a better class of men than of late years have controlled them. In my speeches during the last two years, I have constantly urged the idea that without more attention by our best men to their respective party organizations, good government, especially in a great city like this, is impossible. All my friends know how great is my repugnance to an active personal connection with city politics, even in a temporary and exceptional period. After sixteen months of engrossing occupation, in the various controversies which grew out of the municipal frauds, and the reform in the judiciary, I consider the work I undertook, so far as within my power, to be substantially accomplished. Except in such matters as concerned that work, from the day of the election, I have been totally withdrawn from political action or thought. In that, I am still ready to co-operate as well as in any new legislation necessary for the city. But my attention has been occupied in repairing the long neglect of my private affairs, and in getting ready to execute a purpose which, for some years, has been perfectly settled, and which no vicissitude in State or National politics could have changed. This is a period of relaxation in which to renovate my health by repose and travel. The purpose, and the motive for which I have deferred it for two years, were stated in the following passage from my speech at the Cooper Institute, November 2d, 1871, as it is reported in the *Evening Post:*

"For myself I would gladly have escaped the burden that has fallen upon me. I would have preferred to pass next year and this Winter abroad, to have some repose after twenty years of incessant labor in my profession. It was because I could not reconcile myself to consent that this condition of things should exist without redress, that I deemed it my duty, before I should finally withdraw from public affairs, to make a campaign, to follow where any would dare to lead, to lead where any would dare to follow, in behalf of the ancient and glorious principles of American free government."

"And, by the blessing of God, according to the strength that is given to me, if you will not grow weary and faint, and falter on the way, I will stand by your side until not only civil government shall be reformed in the City of New York, but until the State of New York shall once more have a pure and irreproachable judiciary, and until the example of this great State shall be set up to be followed by all the other States."

OCCASION OF THIS EXPOSITION.

I have deemed this exposition due to Mr. Havemeyer, to the Committee of Seventy, and the other honorable citizens who are striving for good legislation at Albany. It is called for by the elaborate and studied attempt to alarm the party passions of the Republicans by ascribing to me acts and purposes which I have never entertained; and to excuse to the consciences of men who have some hesitating sense of duty, the continuance and renewal of the system of disposing of the great trusts of this city by secret arrangements, carried out by artfully worded legislation at Albany, which is generally obtained by dividing up offices as bribes; of denying the people of this city any voice in their own government, by rendering elections nugatory; and even refusing to the non-partizan Reform Mayor Havemeyer any power over the government he is set to reform. And I now declare that, in all the long diatribes of the *Times,* so far as they relate to me, my plans, designs, purposes, or acts, in respect to Mayor Havemeyer, there is not one word of truth.

Having resolved to depict me as the Mephistopheles, whose influence over Mayor Havemeyer was to alarm the Republicans into seizing away from him the legitimate powers of his office, the *Times* states a variety of pretended facts illustrative of its theory.

In its latest article, it says : " Mr. Tilden, having very carefully held aloof from the contest, and systematically thrown cold water upon it, until he saw it was practically over," * * * " he went about declaring that the *Times* would be beaten, that Mr. Tweed 'carried too many guns for us.'"

The truth is, I never "declared," and never said any such thing, or anything similar, to any human being.

Nor did I "systematically," or at any time "throw cold water" on the contest. How early I took part in it will be discussed hereafter.

It is not true that I had any connection with the Cincinnati nominations. The statement that no one has been able " to extract" from me " a dime towards" the Greeley statue, is equally unfounded. I was never asked but once, and made a subscription on the spot without a word of objection.

I mention these cases as specimens of the loose statements affirmed as positive facts with which these articles abound. I submit to the gentlemen who manage the *Times* that they go beyond the license of legitimate controversy.

Having now disposed of these preliminary matters, I proceed to reply to the substantial allegations contained in the numerous articles of the *Times:*

They are embodied in the following specimen extracts:

MR. TILDEN TOOK NO PART IN THE BATTLE WITH THE " RING."

" The publ c will never forget that, in the greatest battle ever fought with organized corruption in this country, the old Democratic leaders of New York had not the courage or honesty to strike a blow."

" In ALL *that bitter* contest, when at times it seemed as if this Journal would be overwhelmed by its enemies, or at least severely injured by their machinations, we never had a word of open encouragement or an act of assistance from the ancient chiefs of the Democracy."

MR. TILDEN CAME IN ONLY AFTER THE RING WAS DOWN.

" They denounced when it was no longer dangerous to denounce. Then, indignation concerning the " Ring " was most edifying. AFTER " *the king*" was DOWN."

" Mr. Tilden come with his advice when it was very easy to give it, and the other leaders hastened to run from the sinking ship."

"Mr. Tilden was shrewd enough to see that, unless a section of the Democratic Party cut loose from Tammany, the whole Party must inevitably go under with Tammany. He cut loose in the very nick of time to save his own reputation."

HE THROWS MUD ON THE GRAVE OF THE RING.

"Just at present it is a comparatively comfortable thing for * * * Mr. Tilden * * * to throw mud on the grave of the Tammany Ring."

CAPTURING THE COMPTROLLERSHIP FROM THE RING FOR THE REFORM MOVEMENT, WASN'T HIS, AND WAS BUT A TRIFLE.

"Mr. Tilden's *coup d'etat* was not peculiarly Mr. Tilden's, and was anything but a wonderful *coup*."

MR. TILDEN DID NOT COLLECT THE PROOFS.

"We cannot, however, agree with *Mr. Hewitt* that to *Mr. Tilden* is due the credit of *proving* charges vaguely made."

TIME OF TRIAL.

"But there was a time, we beg leave to remind these outspoken denouncers of the 'Ring,' when, to attack TWEED or CONNOLLY, meant to attack an enormous and powerful interest, a gigantic corruption, backed by all the power of the Democratic party. * * * Office, and endowment, and honor, were on the side of the successful scoundrels ; every possible promise of money and place was held out to those who would support them, and those who opposed them had to bear a cutting storm of reproach and obloquy."

MR. TILDEN, WITH MR. O'CONOR AND MR. HEWITT, SEEMED TO COVER THE "RING."

"In those days, respectable gentlemen, leading the Democratic party, like Mr. HEWITT and Mr. TILDEN, though despising, from the bottom of their hearts, the thieves in high places, and believing them thorough swindlers, yet never ventured to utter a word against them in public. In fact, to the distant public, their respectability covered the Ring's rascality. Mr. TILDEN, Mr. O'CONOR, and others like them, appeared the pillars of Tammany Hall."

THE TIMES, THE ELDER SOLDIER.

"Our daily incessant attacks upon Tammany began in the Summer of 1870. It was not until a year later that Mr. Tilden, or any leading Democrat, could be induced to lift a finger or utter a word against Tweed and his confederates."

MR. TILDEN BACKWARD AND TIMID.

"Mr. Tilden was throughout this period as quiet as a mouse, or, if he did appear anywhere in public, it was generally in a position which led people to suppose that he was on the side of the Tweed gang. He presided over their convention at Rochester in September, 1870."

* * * *

"We never questioned the fact that Mr. Tilden, all this time in his heart, detested the Tammany gang, but he took care never to say so."

LAST COMPLAINT.

"He came over to our side, and then did his best to keep up appearances for the Democratic party."

"Mr. Tilden generally manages to save himself by these somersaults at the eleventh hour."

"When a crafty man is plotting to do you some injury, he generally becomes your accuser, and charges you with devising the very mischief he is preparing to launch at your head. Thus Mr. Tilden and his friends are already complaining of the rapacity of the Republicans."

ORIGIN OF THE RING.

The "Ring" had its origin in the Board of Supervisors. That body was created by an act passed in 1857, in connection with the charter of that year. The act provided that but six persons should be voted for by each elector—and twelve should be chosen. In other words, the nominees of the Republican and Democratic party caucuses should be elected. At the next session, the term was extended to six years. So, we had a body, composed of six Republicans and six Democrats, to change a majority of which you must control the primaries of both of the great National and State parties for four years in succession. Not an easy job, certainly! The individual man has little enough of influence when you allow him some chance of determining between two parties, some possibility of converting the minority into a majority. This scheme took away that little. It also invited the managers of the primaries to do as badly as possible by removing all restraints.

It is but just to say that the Democracy are not responsible for this sort of statesmanship, which considers the equal division of official emoluments more important than the administration of official trusts or the well-being of the governed. In the Assembly of 1857, of one hundred and twenty-eight members, the Democracy had but thirty-seven; of thirty-two Senators, it had but four; and had not the Governor. In the thirteen years, from 1857 to 1869, it never had a majority in the Senate; in the Assembly but once; and had the Governor but once up to 1869. The Republicans had the legislative power of the State in all that period, as they and their Whig perdecessors had possessed it for the previous ten years.

The Ring was doubly a "Ring." It was a ring between the six Republican and the six Democratic Supervisors. It soon grew to a ring between the Republican majority in Albany and the half-and-half Supervisors, and a few Democratic officials of this city.

The very definition of a "Ring" is that it encircles enough influential men in the organization of each party to control the action of both party machines; men, who in public push to extremes the abstract ideas of their respective parties, while they secretly join their hands in schemes for personal power and profit.

The Republican partners had the superior power. They could create such institutions as the Board of Supervisors; and could abolish them at will. They could extinguish offices, and substitute others; change the laws which fix their duration, functions and responsibilities, and nearly always could invoke the executive power of removal. The Democratic members, who in some city offices represented the firm to the supposed prejudices of a local Democratic majority, were under the necessity of submitting to whatever terms the Albany legislators imposed; and, at length, found out by experience,—what they had not intellect to foresee—that all real power was in Albany. They began to go there in person to share it. The lucrative city offices—subordinate appointments, which each head of department could create at pleasure, with salaries, in his discretion, distributed among the friends of the legislators—contracts—money contributed by city officials, assessed on their subordinates, raised by jobs under the departments, and sometimes taken from the city treasury,—were the pabulum of corrupt influence which shaped and controlled all legislation. Every year the system grew worse as a governmental institution, and became more powerful and more corrupt. The executive departments, gradually swallowed up all local powers, and themselves were mere deputies of legislators at Albany, on whom alone they were dependent. The Mayor and Common Council ceased to have much legal authority, and lost all practical influence. There was nobody to represent the people of the city—there was no discussion—there was no publicity. Cunning and deceptive provisions of law—concocted in the secrecy of the departments, commissions and bureaus—agreed upon in the lobbies at Albany, between the city officials and the legislators or their go-betweens—appeared on the statute book after every session. In this manner all institutions of government, all taxation, all appropriations of money for our million of people, were formed. For many years there was no time when a vote at a city election would, in any practical degree or manner, affect the City Government.

PERIOD OF RING POWER.

The "Ring" became completely organized and matured on the 1st of January, 1869, when Mr. A. Oakey Hall became Mayor. Mr. Connolly was Comptroller two years earlier.

Its power had already become great; but was as nothing compared with what it acquired on the 5th of April, 1870, by an act which was a mere legislative grant of the offices, giving the powers of local government to individuals of the "Ring," for long periods, and freed from all accountability, as if their names had been mentioned as grantees in the bill.

Its duration was through 1869, 1870 and 1871, until its overthrow at the election of November, when it lost most of the Senators and Assemblymen from this city, and was shaken in its hold on the legislative power of the State.

It will be noticed that the first date in the list of county warrants bearing indications of fraud, published by the *Times* in the last of July, 1871—is January 11th, 1869. Of the $11,250,000, embraced in these accounts, $3,800,000 were in 1869; $880,000 in 1870, before April 5th; $6,250,000 in 1870, after that date; and $323,000 in 1871. The thorough investigation made by Mr. Taintor, at my instance, shows the aggregate vastly larger, but does not much alter the proportions, except in 1871. The periods of power and plunder are coincident in time and magnitude.

FORMATIVE PERIOD.

Even before the " Ring " came into organized existence, the antagonism between those who afterwards became its most leading members, and myself, was sharply defined and public. It originated in no motive of a personal nature on my part; but in the incompatibility of their and my ideas of public duty. I distrusted them. They knew that they could not deceive or seduce me into any deviation from my principles of action. As early as 1863, some of them became deeply embittered, because, being summoned by Governor Seymour to a consultation about the Broadway Railroad Bill, I advised him to veto it.

Some years afterwards I accepted the lead of the Democratic State Organization. I did so with extreme reluctance, and only after having in vain tried to place it in hands in which I could have confidence. I had seen the fearful decay of civic morals incident to the fluctuating values of paper money and civil war. I had heard and believed that the influence of the Republican Party Organization had been habitually sold in the lobbies—sometimes in the guise of counsel fees, and sometimes without any affectation of decency. I had left the Assembly and Constitutional Convention in 1846, when corruption, in the legislative bodies of this State, was totally unknown, and now was convinced that it had become almost universal. I desired to save from degradation the great party whose principles and traditions were mine by inheritance and conviction; and to make it an instrument of a reaction in the community which alone could save free government. Holding wearily the end of a rope, because I feared where it might go if I dropped it, I kept the State organization in absolute independence. I never took a favor of any sort from these men, or from any man I distrusted. I had not much power in the Legislature on questions which interested private cupidity; but in a State Convention, where the best men in society and business would go, because it was for but a day or two, those with whom I acted generally had the majority.

1869.

I had no more knowledge or grounds of suspicion of the frauds of 1869, as they were discovered three years afterwards, than the *Times* or the general public. But I had no faith in the men who became known as the "Ring," and they feared me. I had no personal animosity; but I never conciliated them, and I never turned from what I thought right, to avoid a collision.

The first impulse of their growing ambition and increased power, was to get rid of me and possess themselves of the Democratic State Organization. Their intrigue for this purpose was conceived and agreed upon in the Winter, at Albany, I knew it, but I did nothing till August. Then I accepted the issue; and they were defeated by seven-eighths of the Convention. The country papers of the Republican Party were full of the subject. The files of the *Times* show that the contest attracted public attention. That these men and I were not in accord, was known wherever in the United States there was the least information on such subjects.

This year was marked by the saturnalia of injunctions and receiverships.

In April and May, in speeches in the Circuit Court of the United States, I denounced the orders granted by Barnard to Fisk against the Pacific Railroad Company, as perversions of the instruments of justice, bearing on their face bad faith. I had reason to believe that Tweed was a partner in this freebooting speculation; and his son was Barnard's Receiver. The contest excited universal attention. My motive in taking the case, with great inconvenience to more important business, was the abhorrence I felt of the prostitution of judicial power which touched the rights and interests and honor of every man in the community; and the consideration, that on being applied to by the Company in its extremity, I had advised that the orders in Barnard's Court, for the seven months previous, were nullities, and the acceptance of that advice seemed to impose on me the obligation to maintain it, as was done successfully.

I declined retainers from Fisk in matters involving no scandal, but in which he had not my sympathy, after he had informed me that he had paid a counsel, during the year, many times the largest fee I had ever received; adding, "we don't want anybody else—we want you."

My open denunciations of the judicial abuses, so frequent at this time, and the general support I had received from the country delegates, I have always believed to be the origin of the reaction by which, instead of a third subject for impeachment, Judge Brady was nominated.

In December, I signed the call for the meeting at which the Bar Association was formed. At that meeting, on the first of February, 1870, upon being called on, I gave utterance to my unpremeditated thoughts, in words which stand, without any change, as they were reported in the official proceedings of that body. They were generally deemed to breathe a tone of defiant independence. Among those thoughts were these:

"If the Bar is to become merely a mode of making money, making it in the most convenient way possible, but making it at all hazards, then the Bar is degraded. (Applause.) If the Bar is to be merely an institution that seeks to win causes, and win them by back-door access to the judiciary, then it is not only degraded, but it is corrupt. (Great applause.)

"Sir, I am as peaceable a man as my friend Nicoll, yet I confess that his words of peace sounded a little too strong in my ears. The Bar, if it is to continue to exist, if it would restore itself to the dignity and honor which it once possessed, must be bold in aggression. (Great applause.) If it will do its duty to itself, if it will do its duty to the profession which it follows, and to which it is devoted, the Bar can do everything else. It can have reformed constitutions, it can have *a reformed judiciary*, it can have the *administration of justice* made *pure* and *honorable*, and can restore both the Judiciary and *the Bar*, until it shall be once more, as it formerly was, an *honorable and elevated calling*. (Applause.)

I may mention, in passing, that at this time judicial reform, of which the *Times* was last year so useful a champion, had not then interested it enough to bring into its columns a full report of that important meeting.

CONTEST OF 1870.

For the first time, in four-and-twenty years, the Democrats had, in 1870, the law-making power. They had in the Senate just one vote, and in the Assembly seven votes, more than were necessary to pass a bill, if so rare a thing should happen as that every member was present and all should agree.

This result brought more dismay than joy to the "Ring." They had entrenched themselves against the people of this city in the Legislative bodies. But the Democratic party was bound, by countless pledges, to restore local government to the voting power of the people of the city. The "Ring" could trade in the lobbies at Albany, or with the half-and-half Supervisors in the mysterious chambers of that Board. They might even risk a popular vote on Mayor, if secure in the departments which had all the patronage, and could usually elect their own candidate. But they had no stomach for a free fight, over the whole government, at a separate election.

Their motives were obvious, on a general view of their human nature. None but the "Ring" then knew that, in the secret recesses of the Supervisors, and other similar bureaus, were hid ten millions of bills largely fraudulent, and that, in the perspective, were eighteen other millions, nearly all fraudulent.

THE SHAM.

A sham was necessary to the "Ring." Moral support was necessary to sustain their imposture. None of the "Ring" ever came near me; but Mr. Nathaniel Sands often called to talk over city reform. He sometimes brought my honored and esteemed friend, Mr. Peter Cooper. They were convinced that the "Ring" had become conservative—were not ambitious of more wealth—were on the side of the tax-payers. There was thought to be great peril as to who might come in, in case the "Ring" should be turned out.

I told Mr. Sands I would shelter no sham. I would cooperate with anybody for a good charter. The light and air of Heaven must be let in upon the stagnant darkness of the city administration. The men to come into office must enter *after* a vote of the people. I did not believe the "Ring" would agree to that. I would agree to nothing else.

The "Ring" did not want any conference with me. They tried their own plan. It failed ignominiously. After it was defeated, none were so poor as to do it reverence.

(ver had the slightest chance of revival without a general support of the Republicans. Not only were three Democratic City Senators against it, but enough Democratic Senators from the country would vote against it, if their votes could be made effective.

OPPOSITION.

During the lull, I had conferences with Mr. Jackson S. Schultz, then President of the Union League Club; Mr. Nordhoff, of the *Post*; Mr. Greeley, of the *Tribune*; Mr. Marble, of the *World*, and many others. I entered into no alliance with the "Young Democracy" for future political power, and for weeks was ignorant even of their meetings. I did accept from Mr. Marble two invitations to attend consultations on a draft of a Charter; and certain fundamental ideas, on which he and I insisted, were conceded. These were a separate Municipal election in each Spring, a new election before the Executive offices should be filled, the subjection of all officers to a practical responsibility, and terms of office which should preserve to each successive Mayor his supervisory powers over the government of which he is the head. These ideas were concurred in by the Union League Club, and by the other gentlemen I have mentioned.

THE CONFLICT.

Suddenly a Charter was sprung by Mr. Tweed, and rushed forward very fast.

I was convinced it would pass. A clerk in one of the public offices came privately to tell me "the stuff had been sent up."

There was a movement to resist it. Mr. Schultz, Mr. Bailey and others were in motion. The Union League Club appointed a committee of fifteen to go to Albany to remonstrate. My co-operation was asked. I had little hope. I expected a large Republican support of Mr. Tweed's scheme. But I thought it right to do the utmost for those who were willing to make an effort. I felt more scorn than I ever remember to have felt for the pusillanimity which characterized the hour. I had no objection to hang up my solitary protest against the crime about to be committed. I made a speech before Mr. Tweed and his Committee of the Senate. An unrevised report was published at the time. It contains the following passages:

"By the *first* appointment of these various officers, *self-government* in the people of the City of New York is in *abeyance for from four to eight years*. Sir, by that bill the appointment of all these officers is to be made by a gentleman *now in office*. It is precisely as if in the bill it had read: Not that the Mayor shall make these appointments, but the INDIVIDUAL who *to-day* fills that office. * * * The act proceeds in the same way in which the acts creating commissions have done. A gentleman is designated who makes these appointments. *To all practical intents and purposes* THEY ARE COMMISSIONS *just as under the old system.* * * * Under the Republican system of Commissioners, the Street Department and the Croton Board have been reserved to the control of the city authorities. They stand, as under the old system, anterior to the time when these Commissions began to be formed. * * * The Mayor has no power over these functionaries, except to impeach them, and all experience has shown that that is a dilatory and insufficient resource, not to be relied on in the ordinary administration of the Government. * * * On the 31st December, by the provisions of this bill, the term of (the Mayor's) office will expire. Then, Sir, what will be the situation of his *successor*? For two years he will have *no power whatever* over the administration of the government of which he is the nominal head. All these functionaries survive him. *Their* terms go beyond *his* term, and he has *not* the power to *remove them*, not the power to *enforce any practical responsibility* as against them. He is a mere cipher. Then, Sir, at the end of two years *another* election takes place, *another* Mayor is *elected*. Still these officers extend their terms clear *beyond his*, the shortest of them being for four years, and the longest of them for eight years, many of them for five. * * * This charter is defective in another respect, in that it makes the election of charter officers coincident with that of the State and Federal officers. The municipal election of a million of people is of sufficient importance to be dealt with by itself, and by so doing you *avoid mixing of municipal interests with State and national interests.* * * * What I object to in this bill is that you have a Mayor without *any executive power ;* you have a *Legislature* WITHOUT LEGISLATIVE POWER ; you have *elections* without ANY *power in the people* to AFFECT *the Government for the period during which these officers are appointed.* It is not a *popular* Government, it is not a *responsible* Government ; it is a Government *beyond the control and independent of the will of the people.* That the Mayor should have real and substantial power is the theory we have been discussing for the last four or five years. It is the theory upon which we have carried on our controversies against our adversaries, and are now here. * * After a period of twenty years, for the first time, the party to which I belong possesses all the powers of the Government. I have a strong and anxious desire that it should make for the city of New York a Government popular in its form. Mr. Chairman, I am not afraid of the stormy sea of popular liberty. I still trust the people. We, no doubt, have fallen upon evil times. We, no doubt, have had many occasions for distrust and alarm ; but I still believe that *in the activity generated by the effectual participation of the people in the administration of the Government,* you would have MORE PURITY *and* MORE SAFETY *than under the system to which we have been accustomed.* It is the *stagnation* of BUREAUS and COMMISSIONS that *evils* and *abuses* are *generated.* The storms that disturb the atmosphere clear and purify it. It will be so in politics and municipal administrations if we will only trust the people."

The bill passed. An intenser animosity than was excited against me in the men who thus grasped an irresponsible despotism over this City, cannot be imagined. Mr. Tweed threatened to Lieut. Gov. Beach that they would depose me from the State Committee; and met the answer: "You had better try it."

REAL NATURE OF THE LAW.

Let us pause a moment to consider the real character of that law, fraudulently called a City Charter. Mr. Tweed's case will illustrate its operation. He had never been able to become Street Commissioner. Charles G. Cornell was appointed to that office by a Republican Mayor, and Mr. Tweed made Deputy. When the office became vacant, Mayor Hoffman could not be induced to appoint Mr. Tweed. George W. McLean was appointed, and Mr. Tweed remained Deputy. He had now been turned out as Deputy, and could not get back. On the loss of his office, all his political power turned to dust and ashes.

The Tweed Charter vacated the office of Street Commissioner and of the functionaries of the Croton Department, within five days, vesting all their powers in a Commissioner of Public Works, and required Mr. A. Oakey Hall to appoint that Commissioner. It was known to everybody that Mr. Tweed was to be appointed. The act passed on the 5th, and on the 9th Mr. Tweed was appointed. His term was four years. The power of the Governor to remove him on charges was repealed, and all powers of removal by the City Government. Impeachment was restricted by the condition that the Mayor alone could prefer charges, and trial could only be had if every one of the six Judges of the Common Pleas was present.

ILLUSTRATION.

In ancient times offices were conferred by grant from the sovereign. This was conferred by grant from the State.

Let us suppose the act had run in these words:

"We, the People of the State of New York, represented in Senate and Assembly, do, by our Supreme Legislative authority, hereby grant to William M. Tweed, the office of Commissioner of Public Works; and annex thereto, in addition to the powers heretofore held by the Street Commissioner, all the powers heretofore held by the various officers of the Croton Department, To HAVE AND TO HOLD the same for four years, with the *privilege* of extending the term by surrendering any remnant thereof, and receiving a re-appointment for a *further new term* of *four years*; which office shall be *free* and *discharged* of the power of the Governor to remove for cause on charges, as in the case of Sheriffs, and of all power of removal by the City Government; and absolutely of *all accountability whatsoever*, unless Mayor Hall, or some successor, shall choose to prefer articles of impeachment to the Court of Common Pleas, and unless all the six judges shall attend to try such articles."

I aver that such was exactly the operation of that act. The legal effect and the practical working of the act were identically the same as if it had been expressed in these words.

THE "RING" ENTHRONED OVER THE CITY.

In like manner, the offices of three of the five heads of the Parks were granted for five years to Peter B. Sweeney, Thomas C. Fields and Henry Hilton, giving them the control of the Central Park and every park in the city, and of the Boulevards; suppressing Mr. Green, and removing Messrs. Stebbins, Russell and Blatchford. The office of Chamberlain was granted to Mr. John J. Bradley. The Department of Police was granted for from five to eight years to Messrs. Henry Smith, B. F. Maniere, Bosworth and Brennan. The Departments of Health, Fire, Excise, Charities, Docks and Buildings were granted to others. By an amendment passed twenty days later, Mr. Connolly and Mr. O'Gorman were brought into the same category.

Such a concentration of powers over this city was never before held by any set of men or any party as was thus vested in the "Ring."

The true character of this fraudulent measure was at once fully exposed. The issue was made by Messrs. Schultz, Bailey, Varnum, Greeley and others, and by the Union League Club. All the features of the act were pointed out in their resolutions and remonstrated against. They were discussed, condemned and denounced in my speech published at the time. They were ably exposed by the *World*, the *Evening Post*, the *Sun* and the *Tribune*.

THE MEANS.

It would seem incredible that such a violation of the rights of the people, and of all just ideas of government, even if these extraordinary grants had been to the best men in the community, could be passed. No such thing would have been even excusable, unless for a short time as a temporary dictatorship in a public extremity. It was adopted as a permanent measure; and the grant was to men who were the objects of suspicion; who, in little more than a year afterwards, were hunted from human society, as well as from office, are now arraigned by the State in civil and criminal actions.

The air was full of rumors of corruption. The great public trusts, involving the interests, safety and honor of a million of people, had been divided up as bribes. It was everywhere said that the crime had taken a grosser form; and that Senators and Assemblymen had been bought with money to vote for this iniquity. A year later, it was stated in the newspapers, on the authority of Judge Noah Davis, as derived from a well-known member of the lobby, that the price paid to six leading Republican Senators was to each ten thousand dollars for the charter, and five thousand for the kindred bills of the session, and five thousand for similar services the next year.

Shortly after this revelation, while the revolt of forty thousand Democrats in this City was taking its representation away from the "Ring," the Republicans of the interior were re-electing five of these six Senators as their contribution, with many other similar characters, to the "Reform" Legislature. Those five Senators *now* sit in the highest seats of the Grant Republican Sanhedrim at Albany.

The *Times* has for a long while been as "still as a mouse" about them.

WHO BETRAYED THE CITY?

There have been two great battles against the "Ring." The first was in Albany in April, 1870. That was to prevent the "Ring," while only objects of suspicion, from being enthroned in absolute dominion over the people of this city. The loss of that battle made no change possible until the Senate could be changed. The election for Senators did not come until November, 1871. Then was the second great battle—made necessary by the loss of the first.

Who was responsible for that disastrous day, when the beginning of the crimes afterwards discovered was shrouded in darkness and their larger development made possible? Was it Mr. Tilden? Mr. O'Conor? Mr. Hewitt? Did *their* "respectability cover the 'Ring's' rascality," as the *Times* charges?

means of knowledge more than other citizens; but I had sent to Albany a carefully prepared Election Law, which had been examined and approved by leading Republicans of this city. The Republican Senators rejected it, and took Tweed's Election Law with Tweed's Charter. The *Times* boasted over this election law as "by far the more substantial reform of the two." I feel scarcely able to enter into the comparison of the relative merits of the two measures. The "substantial reform" known as the Election Law, was the means by which Mayor Hall acquired such immense power over the inspectors and canvassers, and all the machinery of the elections, that the "Ring" began to think they could get along without the voters. It suppressed the opposition of the practical politicians in the wards, who saw how it was capable of being worked. In the contest of 1871, it discouraged them from joining us more than any other power wielded by the "Ring." In some districts, men of great local influence openly said, it was of no use to run a ticket so long as that power could be exercised against them. The Reformers were generally appalled by it. I had confidence,—because I counted on the intensity of the popular ferment as likely to permeate and weaken all the agencies of the "Ring," and to swell the wave of opposition until it should sweep over all artificial obstructions.

If the value of a thing is to be measured by what it costs, we are thrown back to a statement made to Judge Davis of the price paid to the leading Republican Senators. Five thousand dollars for the Election law, and for Section Four of the Tax Levy, under which the $6,000,000 of the special audit were acquired, was, perhaps, as cheap as ten thousand dollars for the Charter. The agents of the Citizens' Association cost only a few offices. The *Times* threw itself in gratuitously. My defence, if I need one, for not stopping the "Ring" from cheating at elections, is that I tried to do so but could not. I was beaten by the Republican Senators, and the *Times*.

COURT OF APPEALS.

Soon after the disastrous failure to secure self-government for our people, a lawyer of this city came to me, and said that the best thing for me to do was, to endeavor to secure a good Court of Appeals. My recollection is, that the general term for this department, two of the three members which have since been expelled for corruption, had, at that time, just been constituted. I felt that to make civil rights safe in the second and last appeal was of great value; and set about the work. In the meantime, a distinguished gentleman from the interior, came to propose to me to run as Chief Judge of the new court, and to assure me of a support, which I understood would carry with it the State administration and everything, jealous of or hostile to me throughout the State. It was evident that I was considered less dangerous at the head of the Court than at the head of the State Committee. I answered that I thought I should not be dependent on any such help if I desired the nomination; but that it was not in accord with my plan of life to desire or take the office. I did issue a private appeal for the formation of a good court to nearly all the Democratic lawyers of the State, and to other prominent men. Many of the foremost members of the bar came to the convention, and we nominated and elected five of the seven members of a court which has the complete confidence of the bar and the people. After the judicial election I went on business into distant States until late in the Summer.

WINTER OF 1871.

I did not set my foot in Albany during the session of 1871. The *Times* frequently said, "*Such men as Mr. Samuel Tilden have no real influence.*" If the *Times* meant no influence in what was then the political and legislative Sodom of the State, there is no exaggeration in the assertion. Men who are bought on great questions are in no situation to disobey on inferior matters which are really insisted on. Mr. Tweed was never so supreme over nearly the whole body of the Republican members; and, with their aid, could despise, or suppress and punish, every revolt on the Democratic side. And he had acquired the prestige of successful power. The Democrats had not in either house, one vote to spare from the number necessary to pass a bill. But Mr. Tweed was no worse off that he was completely dependent on his alliances with the Republicans. Nearly every bad measure passed without any opposition, or with only a sham opposition. The *Times*, on one occasion, complained that the root of the evil was in the apathy of the Republican party of the city. There was force in the statement. The prejudices, the party passions, the interests of ambitious men, make the opposition the natural organ of the discontents of society with the ascendant power, which at this time had some pretext for calling itself Democratic, though, in truth, it was a " Ring " of both parties. The combination had such control over the Republicans at Albany and in this city, that a revolution in the Republican party was necessary to create an opposition ; and, without an opposition, dissenting Democrats were powerless. In stimulating the party animosity of the Republicans, even though by vague appeals, or if for merely partisan ends, the *Times* rendered valuable service in a preparation for the future. But time was necessary.

It is wholly untrue that at any moment I was timid, or selfishly reserved, or shrank from any responsibility.

I am not a newspaper whose business it is to address the public every day ; whose recurring want more than meat or bread is a topic ; and to whom invective, even if without facts or evidence, provided it makes a sensation, is money—more money, in circulation and advertisements. Men not of the editorial avocation have to turn from their ordinary duties and habits when they appear before the public, and it is only on few occasions that they find the forum or the opportunity or the leisure. How many times did Mr. William A. Booth, who is mentioned with commendation by the *Times*, and is truly an excellent citizen, or Mr. Jackson Schultz, or even Mr. Evarts, appear during this period ? I will not ask about the Chairman of the Republican State Committee. It is safe to conjecture that he was running of errands for some branch of the "Ring," and serving around the legislative halls for what are daintily termed Counsel fees.

I would have had a perfect right to wait until that "Ring" dominion over our million of people, which the *Times* boasted was "as much" the work of "the Republicans" as of the "Tweed Democracy," had matured its fatal fruits, before I should again renew the battle which had been once betrayed and lost. But, nevertheless, on some occasions I did intervene.

SCHOOL SYSTEM.

The revolution in the School system in the winter of 1871, was the favorite scheme of the master spirit of the "Ring." I publicly condemned it.

CODE AMENDMENT.

The provision of the Code Amendment bill which conferred on the Judges a transcendant authority to punish for what they might choose to consider as contempts, was the measure which was to apply coercion to the press and to speakers who should attack the "Ring." What the two millions a year of advertisements, open to be given or recalled at the will of Mayor Hall, should fail to win, this summary power,—since understood to have been devised by Cardozo, and designed to be wielded by him and Barnard,—was to conquer. It was said— I know not with what truth—to be specially aimed at the *Times*. Probably many an article of that journal in the Spring of 1871, which seemed to the public to be vague and wanting in definite facts, had point enough to the men who knew they had stolen fourteen millions since it helped them into power. At any rate, this scheme was the desperate resource of a domination, bold and blind, as it was ripening for a fall. In it were concentrated the fears and hopes of the "Ring." It was passed without a dissenting voice in either house. Every Republican member voted for it or staid away. The Chairman of the Committee of Conference, who manœuvered it through, was a Republican Senator, who admitted last year the "borrowing" in one instance of $10,000 from Mr. Tweed, which had not been repaid.

One evening in May, when I was temporarily confined to my house by illness, Mr. Randolph Robinson called to ask me to be Chairman of a Committee of the Bar Association to go to Albany and remonstrate with Governor Hoffman against his signing this bill. I declined to be Chairman, but assented that the meeting might put me on the Committee, if it chose to do so, with the knowledge that I could not go; and said that I would write a letter against the bill.

On second thought, a hurried note was addressed to Mr. Evarts, who was Chairman, that it might be sure of publication. It was paraded in the foreground of the controversy. It, and its writer, were constantly cited by the *Times*. An issue was publicly declared from which everybody knew I would not retire. If the bill had not been vetoed, an open collision must have spread all over the State. After I had taken my position, I received assurances of co-operation, in such a controversy, from Francis Kernan and others.

THE CONTEST OF 1871.

The 7th of November, 1871, was the first day when a vote of the people could even indirectly retrieve the results of the legislation of April 5th, 1870.

STRONG POSITION OF THE "RING" IN THE CITY.

Mr. Tweed was in his office until April, 1874; Connolly until 1875, and Sweeney until 1875. They, with the Mayor, were vested with the exclusive legal power of appropriating all moneys raised by taxes or by loans, and an indefinite authority to borrow. Practically, they held all power of municipal legislation, and all power of expending as well as of appropriating moneys. They had filled the departments with their dependants for terms equally long.

They wielded the enormous patronage of offices and contracts. They swayed all the institutions of local government —the local judiciary—the unhappily localized portion of the State judiciary, which includes the Circuit Courts, the Oyer and Terminers, the Special Terms and the General Terms; in a word, everything below the Court of Appeals. They also controlled the whole machinery of Elections. New York City—with its million of people—with its concentration of vast interests of individuals in other States and in foreign countries—with its conspicuous position before the world—had practically no power of self-government. It was ruled, and was to be ruled so long as the terms of these offices continued—from four to eight years—as if it were a conquered province. The central source of all this power was Albany. The system emanated from Albany. It could only be changed at Albany.

In my speech at the Cooper Institute in 1871, I said :

"They stripped every legislative power and every executive power, and all the powers of government, from us ; and vested them in half a dozen men for a period of from four to eight years, who held and were to hold supreme dominion over the people of this city."

"I heard my friend Mr. Choate say that the men in power had been elected by your suffrage. I am sure that was a slip of the tongue. The men in power were elected by no man's suffrage. *They never could have been elected by any man's suffrage.* They were put in power by the Act of the Senate and Assembly of the State of New York, without consulting us or any of us. The ground that I had taken is, that as the *State had put these men on us*, the State *must* TAKE THEM OFF. That is the reason I differ from my Democratic friends of the rural districts, who say :

"What, will you carry a local controversy into the State Convention ? Will you carry it into the politics of the State, and distract and disorganize the Democratic party ?"

I answered, "It is too late to consider that question. For ten years the Democratic party has pledged itself to give back to New York the rights of self-government, and when it came into power it betrayed that pledge and violated that duty."

"Alone I went to the City of Albany, and recorded my protest against the outrage."   *   *   The plan was cunningly contrived and skillfully executed ; but owed its success to a disregard of all moral obligations and all restraints of honor or principle. How was it accomplished ! By taking a million of dollars, stolen from the tax-payers, and buying in the shambles a majority in the two Houses of the Legislature.

"When I spoke against this charter before a Committee of the Senate, Mr. Tweed sitting in the chair, I already knew that not more than one vote of the Democrats and not more than one vote of the Republicans would be cast against it; but I felt it to be my duty to the people of New York, and to the Democratic party, to record my protest against what I then deemed a crime against us, and a betrayal of our principles."

The officers composing the "Ring" government of this city could not be removed, or their power curtailed or limited, except by new legislation. Such legislation could only be made by the concurrent action of the Assembly, Senate and Governor.

If they could hold enough of the Senators to defeat the passage of a bill changing this state of things, they could resist public opinion, and defy the vote of the people of this city, which might spend itself, without results, upon Aldermen and Assistants, totally without power; and on a Mayor, having little legal authority, and capable of being nothing more than a subordinate instrument of the executive departments.

CRISIS OF THE CONTEST.

The Senators who had voted on the 5th of April, 1870, with but two dissenting voices, to create this state of things, did not come within the reach of the people until the election of the 7th of November, 1871, when their successors were to be chosen.

The 5th of April, 1870, and the 7th of November, 1871, were the two days of battle. The intervening time was but the interval between two battles. The period which preceded the election of the 7th November, 1871, was important and valuable only as a time of preparation.

PIVOT OF THE CONTEST.

The objective point of the battle was the legislative power of the State,—the Senators, and Assemblymen.

"RING" PLAN OF THE CAMPAIGN.

The "Ring" saw that. Early there came to me prominent gentlemen from the interior to propose that I should name all the delegates to the State Convention to be sent by the Tammany organization; and so have no contest. The object of the "Ring" was to retain the prestige of "regularity" in aid of the election of their nominees as Senators and Assemblymen. If they could hold the five Senators from this city, they had no misgivings about holding the Republican Senators from the country. At last, when I consented to have a conference with one of them on the basis of a resignation of all city offices, and a withdrawal from the Democratic city organization, and all political leadership, the surrender on my terms was refused; and their reliance on *holding the Senate* BY MEANS OF EIGHT REPUBLICAN SENATORS *already secured to Mr. Tweed,—was avowed.*

A passage of my speech at the Cooper Institute, is reported as follows:

"Mr. Tweed's plan is to carry the Senatorial representation from this city, and then to re-elect eight, and, if possible, twelve of the Republican Senators from the rural districts whom he bought and paid for last year, and to control all the legislation that might be presented there in your behalf; and it was, *because I had some misgivings that this might be done* that I thought it was my duty *personally to take the field and help you in this conflict.* (Applause.)

If I had felt that the Republicans *could have carried the thing of themselves*, it would have been *pleasanter* and *easier* for me to *have stepped aside and let them do it.* I felt it to be my duty to the honest masses of the Democracy, and still more to the people—for party is of no value unless it can serve the people faithfully and effectually—to take my stand with the advanced columns of reform and good government—to take my place there and stand or fall with those who gather round me." (Applause.)

MY PLAN OF THE CAMPAIGN.

My plan of the campaign was in a single idea. It was to take away from the "Ring" the Senators and Assemblymen from this city. That was to storm the central stronghold on which their lines rested, while they were extending their operations over the whole State.

Their allies throughout the State in both parties would be rendered powerless, or be dispersed. I feared most their allies in the Republican party. As it was, the Assembly was largely made up of men who had got themselves nominated by the Republicans, in the expectation that Tweed would come back,— and such golden, or rather greenback showers as he had scattered during the two previous sessions, would descend upon them.

Offers of a surrender of all part in the State Convention, and in the State Organization, were continually made in every form; and weighty pressure was brought on me from powerful men all over the State to accept it, and so " save the party." I uniformly asked " *Who is to have the five Senators and twenty-one Assemblymen?*" In a speech at the State Convention, I made this issue. I said that the object of endeavoring to get a recognition of the organization then controlled by the " Ring," or of avoiding its direct repudiation, was "*to go back and nominate twenty-one Members of Assembly and five Senators*, and then to say to the uprising masses of the best intellect and moral worth of the people"—" *if you do not vote this ticket you are out of the Democratic party.*" I denied that the system of organization then in use in the city, had any moral right to be considered regular, or to bind the Democratic masses. I avowed before the convention, that I would not vote for any one of its nominees as Assemblymen or Senators.

In my speech at Cooper Institute, I said, " A great many times that offer was repeated, and everything was tendered me except the Senate and Assembly of the State of New York, but I said that *everything else was of no value for them to give*, and of *no value for me* to take; that the legislation which should be made in respect to the City Government, whatever else I would compromise, *that I could not compromise*, and I WOULD NOT. (Applause.) I told the State Convention—being the nominal head of the Democratic party of this State—for the sake of perfect frankness and distinctness, and in order that I might not be misunderstood— I told them that I felt it to be my duty to oppose *any man who would not go for making the government of this city what it ought to be, at whatever cost, at whatever sacrifice.* If they did not deem that 'regular,' I would *resign as Chairman of the State Committee, and take my place in the ranks of my plundered fellow-citizens*, and *help* them to FIGHT THEIR BATTLE OF EMANCIPATION."

On this issue I staked my political existence and all my party relations throughout the State. I threw myself into the breach, in order to inspire courage in the Democratic masses of the city to break away from the prestige of a pretended but sham "regularity."

HOW TO OVERTHROW THE "RING" IN THE POPULAR VOTE OF THE CITY.

There was a Democratic majority in the city of at least 40,000 or 50,000, if all the honest, and only the honest votes should be polled. The party organization in the city, which had been accepted by the State Convention for years, in preference to the other organizations that had competed with it, had fallen into the complete possession of the "Ring," and had been made a close corporation, within which no contest could be waged against them, so long as they held so vast official power and patronage. All rival organizations, and nearly all spirit of opposition had been crushed out under the operation of the enormous centralized dominion derived from Albany.

The despondency and disbelief in the possibility of carrying the election in the city against the nominees who would be in the interest of the "Ring" was deep, almost universal and hopeless.

It is seldom that ten per cent. of any party scratch the regular ticket.

To the Democratic masses it was said, not only that the accused persons were innocent, but that even if they were guilty, a great organization ought not to be destroyed for the wrong of a few individuals; that the party was not responsible for them; and that the particular nominees were good men.

How were the votes of twenty or thirty or forty thousand rank and file Democrats to be detached?

Nothing short of an organized revolt of the Democratic masses, under the best Democratic lead, with the most effective measures, and with some good fortune, could accomplish so difficult a work against such extraordinary powers as were combined to uphold the existing system.

The first measure necessary was to break the prestige of the organization which the "Ring" controlled as the representative of the party in the eyes of its masses ; to do this by the act of the State Convention.

That was no easy matter. To able men who sympathized with me it seemed impossible. It proved even more difficult than I expected. A party in power is naturally disposed to risk the continuance of abuses rather than to hazard the extreme remedy of "cutting them out by the roots." The executive power of the State and all its recently enlarged official patronage were exerted against such a policy. And since the contest of 1869, the "Ring" had studied to extend its influence on the rural districts, and had showered legislative favors as if they were ordinary patronage. Without having, or having had for years, the power to give an office in city or State, I stood on the traditions of the older leaders, and the moral sense of the honest masses of the Democratic party.

THE TIME WHEN I ACTED.

The publication by the *Times* of what is called the "Secret Accounts" was completed on the 29th of July. They consisted of copies, made by a clerk, of entries in a book kept in the office of the Comptroller. They showed the dates and amounts of certain payments made by the Comptroller, with a brief description of the objects, and the names of the persons to whom the payments were made.

The enormous amounts, compared with the times and purposes, and the recurrence of the same names, created a moral conviction of gross frauds, though, of course, not amounting to judicial proof against anybody, on which a criminal or civil action would lie, or disclosing the real principals in the fraudulent transactions.

I soon became satisfied of the substantial truth of these statements, by the futility of the answers on behalf of the city officers, and by cross-examining a financial gentleman who came to me with a letter from a distinguished citizen, and the form of a call for a public meeting, which he wished me to head. The statements made me believe that municipal frauds had been committed immeasurably transcending anything I had ever suspected; and they furnished a sort of evidence capable of acting strongly upon the popular mind. I am a believer in the potency of definite facts in making an impression on the public. For that purpose, I had rather have one fact than a column of rhetoric. The publication was made just as I was going into the country. In two or three days there, I formed my programme.

MR. KERNAN.

For so difficult a movement in the State Convention, co-operation was necessary. The first man I sought was Mr. Francis Kernan. His freedom from all entanglements—whether personal or political, with corrupt interests, or corrupt men—his high standard of public duty; his disinterestedness and independence; his tact and eloquence in debate; his general popularity and the readiness of his District to send him as a Delegate—made him my necessary ally in the State Convention. After much telegraphing, I found he was in Albany on professional business. I went there, and passed a day with him.

It was, I believe, the 4th of August, 1871. That was within six days of the time when the publication of the "Secret Accounts" was completed. It was a month before the 4th of September when the meeting was held, at which the Committee of Seventy was created. It was three weeks earlier than I had moved, in 1869, when my own fortunes were involved in a contest with the "Ring." It was earlier than a political campaign in reference to the November election usually opens. It was more than three months before the election. So far from the "battle" being over, it was scarcely begun. So far from the "Ring" being "down" as the *Times* alleges, it was confident of holding its own for months afterwards.

The programme then submitted to Mr. Kernan embraced everything which has been done since, except the impeachment of the Judges. He was about to go to the sea-shore with a sick relative, and while his concurrence was given, particular measures were left for his consideration until his return. Ten days afterward I joined him at Albany—went with him to Utica—and received the assurance of his cooperation; and had consultations with Gov. Seymour, who was also in full sympathy with us. Mr. Kernan will recall the fact that at that first interview—contemplating the difficulty of the conflict—I said and he agreed that we ought to make the contest, even if we should fall in it.

On my way home, I stopped a few days at Saratoga. There I met Mr. George Jones, of the *Times*. I had known him twenty years. He spoke freely to me. I saw no indication that he thought the battle was over. He seemed, rather, to feel its stress. I told him I should appear in the field at the proper time. Often afterwards, when I met him, he referred to that casual interview with apparent satisfaction.

Some five or six weeks later—after Mr. Green was in as substitute for Mr. Connolly, I went into the Comptroller's office. There sat Mr. Jennings and Mr. Jones. The former said, "We want an interview with you." Mr. Green kindly gave us a room in the basement. When we had arrived there, and were seated, Mr. Jennings said: "Do you see any daylight?" and went on to say, in words which I may not be able literally to repeat, that the contest was too exhausting to be continued very long. I stretched out my hand to him, and said: "Be of good cheer! We shall win this fight."

MR. OSWALD OTTENDORFER.

At Utica, I had seen some gentlemen who professed to represent Mr. Ottendorfer's views. I hastened to see him as soon as I arrived at New York. He had accompanied me to Albany the year before, when I made the speech against the Tweed charter. He was a very important element in the contemplated movement. His purity and elevation of purpose made me think he would join us, notwithstanding the great efforts which were made to prevent it. He did so.

MR O'CONOR.

Averse to engaging personally in politics; at an eminence in professional renown—in social consideration—and in personal character, which lifted him above rivalries, and disposed everybody to defer to him, so long as he abstained from fresh collision; entitled to consult his ease and the comfort of tranquility;—Mr. O'Conor was, nevertheless, in complete sympathy with the right. I had often communed with him over evils which, there seemed to be, at the time, no means to redress. I went out to Washington Heights to see him. I told him the hour had come. He said he would help according to his view of what he was best adapted to, and of what was most fit for him to undertake.

There were great legal difficulties in the way of getting investigation or redress.

The Aldermen, who were vested with a statutory power of compelling disclosure, were allies of the "Ring." The Legislature was not in session. For a long time there was no grand jury, capable of making the traditionary inquest, which had not been packed.

The local authorities which had power to order civil actions, if such would lie in their behalf, were in complicity with the wrong-doers. The officials who would conduct such actions were their appointees; the juries would be selected in their interest, and the Judges who dominated in the Courts were their instruments.

Criminal proceedings were equally hampered.

Well might the Mayor say to Garvey—as the latter has recently testified—"who is to sue?"

As early as August, I had discussed with Mr. O'Conor the right of the State by the Attorney-General to sue; but even that resource was unavailable, because we could not then count on the co-operation of that officer.

When I suggested a new law appointing one or three Commissioners; conferring on them full powers of compelling disclosure; vesting them with the right to sue; enabling them to lay the venue outside of this county; giving preference to their actions; with other provisions to render the remedy speedy and efficacious,—Mr. O'Conor said he would take the head of such a Commission.

It was these conferences which led Mr. Kernan and myself to vote for Mr. O'Conor—without his knowledge—as Attorney-General. To the gentleman who was nominated, I sent a message advising him of the necessity that he should satisfy the people of New York that he would exert the powers of his office in their behalf. He came to my house on the Sunday morning of October 15th, with a letter dated the 14th, which was published on the 16th, containing such an assurance; and said he would authorize any suit Mr. O'Conor or I should advise. He had returned to Albany and communicated this agreement to Gov. Hoffman, before the Delegates of the Committee of Seventy had their interview—on the afternoon of the 17th—at which Mr. Champlain announced his purpose to depute Mr. O'Conor.

With characteristic disinterestedness and public spirit, that trust was undertaken by Mr. O'Conor, with the declaration that he would accept no compensation for his professional work; and ever since, he has given his time and his great abilities and acquirements to the service of the people.

OTHER PREPARATIONS.

These conferences were in August, and before the Committee of Seventy was appointed. They did not wait for or depend upon any co-operation. They contemplated independent action. Other preparations for the State Convention were made. I accepted an arrangement to be upon the floor as the representative of my native district, which had always during the "Ring" ascendancy, provided me that opportunity. I asked a few other gentlemen to come, but had not time to look after Delegates in detail. I did, however, early in September, issue a letter to 26,000 Democrats, reviewing the situation, and calling upon them to "take a knife and cut the cancer out by the roots."

SUBSTITUTION OF MR. GREEN FOR MR. CONNOLLY IN THE COMPTROLLERSHIP.

Meantime an important event happened which could not have been foreseen.

On the 14th of September, Mr. Connolly applied to me through a friend for an interview. Without knowing its object, I gave it on the morning of the 15th. The most artful members of the "Ring" plotted to save themselves—to come in as parts of a new system—even as reformers—with added power—upon Connolly's ruin. In his distrust of them and fears for himself, he sought advice.

I began by telling him that I could not be his counsel or assume any fiduciary relations toward him; that he and all the others must surrender all office and all local party leadership; and recognize the fact that their careers were ended.

To this he assented; but still wanted my advice. I counselled him that he had no right to resign his office into the hands of his confederates; that such an act would be a new wrong against the public.

To his inquiry, whether if he remained he could get money to carry on the government, I told him I would consult Mr. Havemeyer, and we would meet him again that evening.

Mr. Havemeyer came, but Connolly did not. After consultation, Mr. Havemeyer went to Connolly's house; found him in bed, sick; encouraged him; appointed a meeting at my house for the next morning at ten; and requested, as I had desired, that Connolly's counsel should come with him.

Meantime, I had examined the law and found a singular enactment, by which the Comptroller was authorized to appoint a deputy, and confer upon him for a definite period all his own official powers. Mr. Havemeyer must have been informed of this, and consulted about the proposed action under it before he went to Connolly's, for he had agreed to assume the responsibility of public advice to Connolly to stay in, as Mr. Green could only hold as his deputy. Besides Mr. Havemeyer and Mr. Green, the only human being who had any intimation of the purpose was Judge Swayne, of the Supreme Court of the

United States, who passed the evening with me, to whom I confided the matter, with whom I discussed the question of the right of the State to sue in such cases under the general rules of jurisprudence, and, in the intervals of conversation with whom, I prepared some of the papers.

In the morning, Mr. Havemeyer and Mr. Connolly and his counsel came. I pressed Mr. Connolly to surrender the office into the hands of the Reformers by deputing Mr. Green to exercise all its powers; that he had less to fear from the public than from his confederates; that if he threw himself upon the mercy of the public, and evinced a disposition to aid the right, the storm would pass him and beat upon the others. His counsel said it was a personal question. One of them stated the opposite view taken by some of Mr. Connolly's friends. It was, that if he would resign, a man should be put in his place who would have character enough to assume the whole duty of investigation and would exclude the committee of which Mr. Booth was chairman, and that Mr. Connolly should be protected. It was disclosed that the counsel who presented this view had come fresh from an interview with Mr. Sweeney.

At length Mr. Connolly consented, the papers were executed, Mr. Green sworn in, and they left my house only to go to the office of the Comptroller and put Mr. Green in possession.

The *Times* seems to consider the acquisition of this office by the Reformers at that stage of the contest as of little value. That was not its opinion at the time. It is not my opinion.

The possession of the Comptrollership by the Reformers was a fatal embarrassment to the "Ring." It involved a publicity of all the expenditures of the departments; and was a restraint on those expenditures. It created doubt and dismay in all their action. It was an obstacle to such modes of raising money as had brought the charter through in 1870; and to the hope of reimbursing advances for such purposes. It protected the records on which all civil and criminal actions must be founded, from such destruction as was attempted in the burning of the vouchers. Every investigation, including that of

Mr. Booth's committee, were fruits of that possession. So also was the discovery of judicial proofs, in the Broadway Bank; and the collection of such proofs which continued for eight months afterwards, with important results which have not even yet become public. It divided the influence of the city government in the elections, and broke the prestige of the "Ring."

EFFORTS OF THE "RING" TO RECOVER POSSESSION.

Then began a struggle on the part of the "Ring" to force Mr. Connolly to resign, in order that Mr. Green's powers might cease. On the 18th, the Mayor treated Mr. Connolly's deputation of Mr. Green as a resignation; and then, with singular inconsistency, assumed to remove Mr. Connolly, though he had lately declared he had no power of removal. The vacancy thus alleged to exist, he, on two incompatible theories, each totally unfounded, proceeded to fill.

Early that morning I sought Mr. O'Conor. The freedom from doubt of the law was no security. The moral support of his great legal name, affirming the validity of Mr. Green's possession, was necessary. He examined the statutes, and had no doubt. He consented to reduce his opinion to writing, saying that he would not take a fee, and inserting the explanation that the opinion was given at my request. It appeared in the *Evening Post* of that afternoon.

An attempt, under color of judicial process, to forcibly eject Mr. Green, was anticipated. A carriage was waiting to take me to Judge Brady. If a Judge could be found to vacate fraudulent orders, as fast as they could be granted, it was well. If not, I had resolved the next day to open an issue, in advance of the election of the new Legislature—a Convention to revise the judiciary.

Mr. O'Conor's opinion saved that day. Mr. O'Gorman, evading the legal question, advised the Mayor, as a matter of expediency, to acquiesce in Mr. O'Conor's opinion. The plot fell to pieces.

But there were men behind the Mayor who would not yet

give up the struggle. When Keyser alleged that his name on the warrants was forged, the effort was renewed. It was in resisting it that I struck on the clue which led to the revelations of the Broadway Bank.

STATE CONVENTION.

The contest in the State Convention quickly followed. It is but fair to admit that what I asked the Convention to do, was more than any party was ever found able to venture upon. It was to totally cut off and cast out from party association, a local organization, which held the influence growing out of the employment of twelve thousand persons, and the disbursement of thirty millions a year, which had possession of all the machinery of local government, dominated the judiciary and police, and swayed the officers of the election. I still think that, on such an occasion, the greatest audacity in the right would have been the highest wisdom, and, in the long run, the most consummate prudence. If the Convention could not reach that breadth and elevation of action, it nevertheless did help to break the prestige by which the organization expected to enthrall the local masses. For myself, I at no time hesitated to avow, as my conviction of duty and my rule of action, that a million of people were not to be given over to pillage to serve any party expediency, or to advance any views of State or National politics.

OTHER ACTION.

For more than three months I devoted myself to this contest. Whatever seemed, on a general survey of the whole field, necessary to be done, I endeavored to find the best men and best methods to do, and, at all events, to have that thing accomplished. I addressed the Democratic masses. I constantly pointed out to the public the legislative bodies as the turning point of the controversy. I entered into an arrangement with Mr. O'Conor and Mr. Evarts to go to the Legislature; and, when events afterwards induced them to abandon the intention, I went alone. I invited the meeting at which the reform delegation to the State Convention was originated, and helped to form that delegation.

On the eve of the election, when Mr. Wickham, who was chairman of the newly extemporized Democratic reform organization, came to me to say that they could not supply booths or ballots without $10,000 beyond what they were able to raise, I agreed to provide it, and did so. With the aid of Mr. Edward Cooper, I raised from personal friends, including my own contributions, for the legitimate purposes of the contest, about the same sum which I understand the Committee of Seventy collected from the whole community for similar purposes.

BROADWAY BANK INVESTIGATIONS.

These investigations furnished the first, and, for a long time, the only judicial proof of the frauds. They occupied me, and some four or five clerks and assistants, about ten days. The analysis of the results, and their application as proof, were made by myself; as well as the original discovery of the relation of the numbers which was the clue to all the revelations.

The *Times* seems to ascribe the collection of judicial proof to Mr. Booth's committee. This is an entire error. Nothing of the kind was attempted by that Committee. The value of their report was in its exhibition of the accounts of payments from the Comptroller's office. It did not trace any share of the money to any public officer. That Mr. Booth was allowed to inspect the accounts was due to the possession of the Comptroller's office by Mr. Green.

This information obtained from the Broadway Bank established the fact that but one-third of the nominal amount of the bills had ever reached the persons who pretended to be entitled to the payments, and that two-thirds had been divided among public officers and their accomplices; and it traced the dividends into the actual possession of some of the accused parties. It converted a strong suspicion into a mathematical certainty; and it furnishes judicial proof against the guilty parties. On this evidence, and on my affidavits verifying it, the action by the Attorney-General was founded.

SPEECH AT COOPER INSTITUTE.

At the great "Reform" meeting at the Cooper Institute, I made a speech advocating a union of all the elements opposed to the Ring, without reference to State or National politics. This was done while I was the official head of the State organization of the Democratic party. My action was regarded as questionable by some good men who judged it by the ordinary standard of political parties. All the secret allies of the " Ring" throughout the State were employed, aided by most of the executive patronage, in accusing me of sacrificing the success of the State ticket, and the supremacy of the Democratic party in the State to my effort to overthrow the "Ring." Complaints were inspired from high quarters that I had not kept back the Broadway Bank disclosures and deferred the action by the Attorney-General until after the election. This was the basis of an organized movement against me in the Assembly, continued and renewed for a whole year throughout the State. My own opinion was, and is, that the most vigorous and effective measures were necessary to overthrow the corrupt dominion over this city; that if they had not been taken with boldness, the immense power which has been created by the legislation of 1870,—the whole local Government machinery—with its expenditure and patronage, and its employment of at least, twelve thousand persons, and its possession of the police, its influence on the judiciary, its control of the inspectors and canvassers of the elections, would have enabled the " Ring " to hold a majority in the city; and would have defeated all adverse legislation at Albany.

And while I never hesitated to avow that the emancipation of our million of people was not to be made secondary to any other object by a citizen and elector of this city, I thought and still think the timid and false policy I was assailed for not adopting—if I know aright the many high-minded and independent gentlemen of the interior who would not have brooked any compromise with wrong—would have been far more disastrous to the State ticket in that election, and would have permanently compromised the Democratic party. It is to the eternal honor of the Democratic masses of this State that on the issues thus made with me successively for a whole year, they gave me an overwhelming support.

DEMOCRATIC REFORM VOTE IN THE CITY.

How largely the redemption of the city was due to the Democratic masses is easily shown. The vote for Willers, the Democratic candidate for Secretary of State, was 83,326. His majority was 29,189. The vote for Sigel, the Union Reform candidate for Register, was 82,565. His majority was 28,117. Willers' vote was nearly 1,000, and his majority more than 1,000 the larger.

It follows that 28,653 Democrats who voted for Willers, also voted for Sigel. Even that does not show the whole Democratic contribution to the reform victory. For at least, 10,000 or 12,000 democrats—dissatisfied that the State Convention had not gone further than it did—voted the Republican State ticket. The whole Democratic vote cast for Sigel was little short of 40,000, against the 42,500 he received from all other sources. The result—so much more overwhelming than was expected by the public—not only changed the city representation in the legislative bodies of the State, but, in its moral effect, crushed the " Ring."

So far from true is it that the " battle " was " over," as the *Times* alleges when I entered it, the battle was not over till the polls closed. Even to the night before the election, general despondency prevailed. All through the contest, it was difficult to inspire the local politicians with confidence in our chances of success. Many whose sympathies, interests, and resentments were with us held back, and some abandoned us at a late period. The Republicans in the city had little hope.

The belief was general in the City and State, and among all parties, even to the election, that we should fail, and that the " Ring " would hold a majority.

FURTHER COLLECTION OF PROOFS.

After the election, it was urged by Mr. O'Conor, Mr. Havemeyer, and Mr. Green, that I ought to continue the investigations by which the judicial evidence of the frauds should be collected and preserved; that this work was more important than even the preparation of legislation. In deference to their views, I gave my time to the work, during all the six weeks, until the legislative session commenced; and in every interval at my command for many months afterwards. When the investigations commenced, there were no means by which disclosure could be compelled, that were not in the hands of the accused parties, except a grand jury, whose sessions were prolonged for several months. A vast mass of accurate information has been collected and preserved, which is the basis of nearly all judicial proofs that have been obtained.

JUDICIAL REFORM.

It was the opinion of our best men, as it was my own, that a reform in the administration of justice, as it was carried on in this judicial department of the Supreme Court, was not only intrinsically the most important to the welfare, safety and honor of our community, but was a measure, without which every other reform would prove nugatory; and that the opportunity of effecting it at the last session could not be allowed to pass unimproved without leaving us for an indefinate period subject to the intolerable evils and scandals which had recently grown up, and to the world-wide disrepute they had occasioned. As a citizen and a lawyer—trained amid better standards—I had seen the descent of the bench and the bar with inexpressible concern. I had often questioned, with Mr. O'Conor, whether those of us at the bar who had ceased to be dependent for a livelihood upon professional earnings, ought not to feel ourselves under a Providential call, on the first opportunity, to open to the younger members of the profession a better future than that which was closing in upon them—a future in which personal and professional honor would not be incompatable with pecuniary success. I had advised a son of Francis Kernan, who came here to begin a career, to return to Utica rather than confront the degrading competition to which a young man would be exposed. In the heat of an extemporaneous speech, at the Cooper Institute, I had become committed to this cause.

It seemed to me a paramount duty to press a movement for that object with all the concentration and persistence requisite to success; and there never was a moment, by day or night, during all the session, when anything which it was possible to do could be safely omitted. There were several periods of general despondency, and frequent crises in which the cause had to be rescued.

It early came to the knowledge of Mr. Peckham, Mr. O'Conor, and myself, that a large fund was attempted to be raised for the purpose of corrupting the Committee and the Assembly, in the interest of the accused judges. Even after the impeachment was adopted by the Assembly—when general despair was felt at the choice of managers—the lost ground was promptly recovered by a measure initiated by myself. It was an arrangement by which the selection of counsel was to be satisfactory to the Bar Association.

Attention to the completion of this object; to the conduct of the suits which had been commenced; to the gathering in of the fruits of the investigations; and to other accessory work necessary to finish the original undertakings, occupied most of the Summer.

CONCLUSION.

On the whole, I have given sixteen months of time to these public objects, with as incessant and earnest effort as I ever applied to any purpose. The total surrender of my professional business during that period, the nearly absolute withdrawal of attention from my private affairs, and from all enterprises in which I am interested, have cost me a loss of actual income, which, with the expenditures and contributions the contest has required, would be a respectable endowment of a public charity. The surrender of two Summers, after I had shaped all my engagements to take my first vacation in many years, was a serious sacrifice.

I do not speak of these things to regret them. In my opinion, no instrumentality in human society is so potential in its influence on the well-being of mankind as the governmental machinery which administers justice and makes and executes laws. No benefaction of private benevolence could be so fruitful in benefits as the rescue of this machinery from the perversion which had made it a means of conspiracy, fraud, and crime, against the rights and the most sacred interests of a great community.

The cancer which reached a head in the municipal government of the metropolis, gathered its virus from the corrupted blood which pervades our whole country. Everywhere there are violated public and private trusts. The carpet-bag governments are cancers on the body politic, even more virulent than the New York "Ring."

I felt impelled to deal with the evil here, because an offence which is directly before one's eyes is doubly an offence; and because it was within our reach, while to renovate government throughout the United States is a work of great difficulty, taking time, large hope of the future and long continued efforts towards reformation. If the world cannot be changed, it is something to make one's own home fitter to live in.

A reaction must begin somewhere. I have not lost hope that free government upon this continent may yet be saved. I remember that nations have experienced great changes for the better, in manners and in morals, after long periods of decay. There are some good signs in our own horizon. Last month, when a gigantic controversy of the stock market reached the courts, none of the journals enquired, "Which side owns the Judge?" At any time within the last three years, that would have been the only theme.

The money-articles have ceased to treat their readers to admiring discussions of the relative dexterity with which men of colossal capitals—first citizens of the Metropolis—representatives of its monied aristocracy—contend with each other in feats which have a moral aspect about like cheating at cards. Since the swell of the paper money afflatus in 1863, the absence of such discussions is a refreshing novelty at our breakfasts. Even on the cheek of a member of Congress begins to rise a delicate hue of doubt in being discovered to have had a pecuniary interest in a public question on which he has voted. Amid the blackness of successful wrong which overspreads the whole heavens, are these little gleams of a revival of the public conscience. If its growth shall be as steady, as rapid, and as persistent, as has been its decay during the last ten years, everywhere throughout the country will come revolutions of measures and of men.

If the work to which I have given so freely, according to the measure of my abilities, shall stand,—I will not compete for its honors, nor care for falsehood or calumny concerning the part I have borne in it.

If it is to fail once more—if the people of this Metropolis—if the Republican citizens of culture and property, whose interests are deeply involved in a good Municipal Government—and who are now to show whether they will stand against bad measures in their own party, shall shamefully consent to a repetition of the fraudulent devices of the Tweed charter of 1870—theirs, not mine, will be the responsibility.

S. J. TILDEN.

New York, January 27th, 1873.

APPENDIX.

[*While the letter is passing through the press—two notes and a few out of many proofs—are added.*]

THE FOLEY INJUNCTION.

It may be fit to advert to a criticism of the SUN on the omission of my letter to mention the Foley injunction. Certainly this did not arise from any disposition to disparage the activity and zeal so often conspicuously displayed by Mr. Foley in the contest against the "Ring." The idea did not occur to me that this event was pertinent to the line of my discussion. It is possible, also, that the omission may be an unconscious expression of my view of that litigation.

Mr. Foley, as a tax-payer, had no standing in Court to ask for an injunction against Mr. Connolly as Comptroller. The law in this respect had been perfectly settled for years by two leading cases in the Court of Appeals. It was the duty of a Judge who recognized the obligation of deciding according to law, to deny the motion for the injunction; and it would have been the duty of any other Judge, before whom the motion to dissolve it could be brought on, to grant that motion. The Attorney-General, as plaintiff on Mr. Foley's relation, or without a relator, could have maintained an action; but no individual tax-payer was entitled in such a case to represent the public.

If the suit was futile, as a means of lawful redress in the Courts, its value was only as an instrument of popular excitement, or of alarm or embarrassment to the public officers, against whom it was directed. The order to show cause, with a stay, was made Sept. 7th; the motion was heard and the injunction granted on Sept. 15th. In the meantime—on Sept. 10th, —the robbery and burning of the vouchers occurred; and on the 11th, Mayor Hall's letter appeared, demanding the resignation of Comptroller Connolly.

The injunction was specially aimed at Connolly; and he was strongly denounced in Barnard's opinion.

Information at the time, which I think came through Connolly, convinced me that Barnard acted upon consultation with Sweeny. That belief was subsequently confirmed in a manner which left no possibility of doubt.

The Albany plan—which, in my opinion, emanated from Sweeny—had earlier become known to me. It was that "Connolly should be indicted, and Tweed should go to Europe." The idea was given out, that the way was to deal with one at a time. If this purpose was, in good faith, entertained in respect to Tweed, there was never the courage or the ability to carry it into effect; for he had vastly the superior power.

The only reality was in the plot to crush Connolly, and, upon his ruin, to reconstruct the "Ring." For this object, as well as for concealment, the vouchers were stolen and burned, and the crime charged on him; and for this object, also, in my judgment, the injunction and the denunciation in Barnard's opinion were specially levelled against him.

For some time previous there often came to me persons saying that Sweeny was with me. Now and then, in newspaper articles denouncing Connolly, would appear the suggestion that if such men as Mr. Tilden and Mr. Sweeny would come forward, all would be well. Every effort, from the 11th of Sept., had been used to force Connolly to resign. It must have been known to the "Ring" that I did not think his resignation alone would or ought to satisfy the people; for I had so said in Albany the week before. But rumors appeared in the journals associating me with other gentlemen in these negotiations too often to be accidental. So, an interview was accorded to a reporter of the *Times*, which was published on the morning of the 15th, denying any connection with these movements; and adding that "I don't think the medicine is powerful enough for the disease."

The injunction was granted on the afternoon of the 15th. It was on the morning of that day that I gave the interview to Connolly, and advised him not to surrender his office into the hands of his confederates.

It was on the evening of that day that Mr. Havemeyer went from my house to Connolly's, found him sick in bed—"put some back-bone into him," as he said—and arranged the meeting for the next morning at my house, when Mr. Green was substituted. It was on the morning after the injunction that the proposal was made by Sweeney, that a man should be put in who would assume the whole duty of investigation—exclude Mr. Booth's committee—and assure Mr. Connolly of protection.

Mayor Hall's letter to Connolly, removing him, was dated the 18th. His letter to Gen. McClellan, asking his acceptance, was dated the 16th. It had probably been prepared for the event of Connolly's resignation, and the first sentence altered after Connolly's substitution of Green, without changing the date, which was prior to the knowledge of this act, on which the letter was predicated. I never thought that, if Connolly had resigned, Gen. McClellan would have been appointed; for he would not have undertaken the engagements offered to Connolly.

Mr. Sweeney's intrigues to survive his associates, and come up with a reform aspect, as a part of the reconstructed "Ring," must have been founded on the success of the imposture of the "Reformed" charter of 1870, and on his superior skill in concealing his part in the plunder. It took an expert, under my supervision, six months to explore the devious paths by which that share found its way into his possession.

Mr. Foley, of course, was not responsible for the law of the case, or for the use which the survivors of the "Ring" sought to make of his well-intended suit, or of his meritorious endeavors.

THE IMPEACHMENT OF BARNARD.

It was natural that the Bar Association should send their memorial to me for presentation, and the fact that they did so was no disparagement to anybody else. Instead of presenting it, and making it the occasion of a speech, I retained it, and gave it back to the Committee, advising them to take it to Mr. Alvord for presentation. I deemed his co-operation important; thought his parliamentary skill and influence entitled to him a consideration which a section of his own party were not disposed to accord to him; and, for the interest of the cause, felt willing to invite his leadership, and to be myself a follower. Messrs. Van Cott, Judge Davis, Peckham, Barlow, Spier, Carter and others will doubtless recall these circumstances. The Committee had no reason to regret the adoption of my advice. Mr. Alvord gave his co-operation throughout the session and the trial.

On Friday, the 10th of May, the Managers were chosen by secret ballot. The result was, no doubt, caused in part by an eager competition by some for the distinction; and, in part, by an organized effort to give the body a character as little hostile as possible to the accused. While some of the members were cordially accepted by the public—the choice on the whole created general, and, as I thought, excessive distrust, and a despair of the impeachment.

On the Monday morning following—the 13th—a gentleman went to Albany with me; had an interview with Mr. Alvord that afternoon; proposed to him that the Managers should select Judge Comstock as their counsel and such associates as should be satisfactory to the Bar Association—and brought me an assurance of the cordial action of Mr. Alvord for that end. Of course, I do not say that he would not have done the same thing without suggestion.

In a debate which sprang up that evening, I said that I was personally content with an honorable discharge from the duty of a Manager, though I would not have declined that duty; delicately alluded to the question of counsel; and endeavored to reassure the public—expressing my confidence in the action of the Managers, and the result of the trial. The subject was more fully discussed in a speech of mine at a ·meeting of the Bar Association on May 28th. An extract is subjoined.

There is no imputation upon the action of the Managers or of the Judiciary Committee in my letter. Mr. Alvord, Mr. Husted, Mr. Fort, Mr. Lincoln, and others—not members of the Judiciary Committee—had given a steady support to the proceedings.

Mr. Alvord is understood to have moved in the Managers the resolution adopted by them, to commit the whole conduct of the trial to the counsel—which was not the least among his services.

ADDRESS OF SAMUEL J. TILDEN BEFORE THE BAR ASSOCIATION, MAY 28, 1872.

An adjourned meeting of the Bar Association was held at their rooms last night, Mr. Tilden occupying the chair by special invitation. On taking his seat, Mr. Tilden spoke as follows:

* * * * * * *

One word as to the pending impeachment of Judge Barnard. I do not share the fears which have been expressed in the public journals as to the result. *First.* I know that in the investigation which extended to all the witnesses the accused desired to produce, and with full cross-examinations, there was developed more impeachable matter—ten times over—than can be found in the eight principal cases of judicial impeachment—four resulting in convictions—which have occurred in this country. *Secondly.* I believe that the leading members of the Committee of Managers will faithfully prosecute the trial. *Thirdly.* I have the most absolute confidence in the abilities, professional skill, and earnest patriotism of the counsel who will represent the people, and on whom the real burden of the trial will fall.

I respect the sentiments of my brethren of the Bar, which demanded that I should continue still further my connection with the movement to purify the judiciary. I mean, of course, as one of the managers of the impeachment, for you all know that I would not have acted as counsel. While I did not feel at liberty, by my own act, to withhold any service which you thought I could render to the great Reform, my opinion differs somewhat from the public impression. The great work of investigation ; of collecting evidence, and of securing sufficient concurrence and co-operation to put the accused on trial, which has been an immense and difficult labor—is done. The gentlemen whom I met in conference, after everything had been completed except to decide on the form of procedure, when I consented to impeachment instead of removal, by concurrent resolution—and I see several of those gentlemen present—will remember that I then stated my difficulty in engaging in a prolonged trial during the Summer.

When the choice of managers came to be made I did not feel called on to enter into a canvass or to form combinations. In everything else I had felt it my duty to exercise all foresight, and every care, and to exert whatever power I possess to organize such elements as could be found for good ends. In this, I felt entitled to leave every human being in the Assembly to his spontaneous action. If I should receive an honorable discharge, I had a right to accept it. I cannot be accused of selfishness if I did so with delight. One care only remained for me, that was, to look after the choice of counsel. I *communicated what seemed to be*, in the actual circumstances, *the best suggestions* to *Mr. Alvord*, and met his *prompt* and *cordial concurrence*.

I do not see that justice will be more likely to fail, that the trial is to be conducted in the light of open day, with the eager scrutiny of the Bar of the State and country, and under the eyes of a *watchful*, apprehensive, and *somewhat distrusting people*.

While, what has been done toward purifying the judiciary, is just cause of congratulation, you will appreciate the difficulties through which it has been obtained, if you reflect that everything else, in the way of Reform, has failed. It is known to you that when I consented to go to the Assembly, it was with a view to the judicial reform, and to certain other measures, more particularly interesting the people of this city; and that, in that work, I expected the co-operation in the Legislature of Mr. O'Conor and Mr. Evarts. This arrangement was defeated by subsequent events. I believed that it was necessary to concentrate myself upon a very few measures, in order to accomplish anything.

The general demoralization, growing out of the civil war and paper money, had produced wide-spread effects. The corrupt power which had just been overthrown in this city had its origin in a partnership of plunder between men nominally of different politics, but, in fact, of no politics at all; and had established extensive affiliations throughout the State, in both parties, and in both branches of the dominant party, which now possessed three-quarters of the Legislature. It had been necessary to the system, that the Capitol should be surrounded by an atmosphere of corruption. The ambition of some had been tempted; the interests of more had been addressed by making legislative business profitable, and the golden showers had sprinkled benefits in every direction. Some, even, who would not take an actual part in the saturnalia, were content to be silent spectators or consenting witnesses. I never, for a moment, supposed that the knife and the cautery would be agreeable remedies, or that the silent partners of prosperous criminals, would fall in love with those whose duty it is to detect and punish. I knew, therefore, that obstructions, under every pretext, were to be met at every step, and to be overcome.

[*From the Tribune of Feb. 7th*, 1873.]

MR. TILDEN'S ATTITUDE DURING COMPTROLLER GREEN'S FIRST WEEK IN OFFICE.

A *Tribune* reporter called on the Hon. Samuel J. Tilden, last evening, to inquire about the interview between him and the editor of *The New York Times*, of which an account was given in Tuesday's issue (Feb. 4th) of that journal, quite at variance with the statements made by Mr. Tilden in the letter recently published. The reporter called Mr. Tilden's attention to the following extract from the editor's statement:

Mr Tilden is a great man, but we never asked for an interview with him. Mr. Green requested us to see him. We consented; and we *then* and *there* told Mr. Tilden *plainly* that it was time he and the other Democratic leaders *let the public know* on *which side* THEY were prepared to fight; that there was *disgraceful* for them to *remain silent*; that he (Mr. Tilden) must not expect to escape censure *any longer* if he *still refused to join* in the attack on Tammany. For the managers of this journal to have said that the fight was "exhausting," at the very time when victory was within easy reach, would have been manifestly absurd. No such words were ever uttered—even Mr. Tilden guards himself against positively asserting that they were. Those who know Mr. Tilden, and those who know the managers of this journal, can judge for themselves which of them were the most likely to need encouragement. Mr. Tilden was *remonstrated* with in earnest language upon *his inaction*; *he begged* that the interview might be kept *secret*; and he breathed forth, in a mournful undertone, a *promise* to put on his armor and enter the field without delay. Mr. Tilden must have dreamt since that he was suddenly transformed, on that afternoon, into another Hercules. In reality, he seemed to be afraid of his own shadow. He appeared to think that Tweed was waiting for him at the door. *His voice was never raised above a lover's whisper.* It was not until success was assured, by the results of the November election, that the intrepidity of his soul revealed itself. After that he did good service—we have never denied it.

Mr. Tilden replied : I did not have time to read the article fully, till this evening. I came home tired, and, after resting myself, I read the account of this interview. It is very funny. * * *

TIME AND PLACE OF INTERVIEW.

Now, observe the *place* and the *time* of this interview. It was in a basement room of the New Court House, given us by Mr. Green *after* he had become installed as a substitute for Mr. Connolly. The time will be seen, by computation, to be the second week of Mr. Green's possession of that office, or later. The first week was occupied by the contest on my part to keep him in, and on the part of the Ring to drive him out, and with controversies connected with it.

DATE OF MR. GREEN'S ENTRY.

Mr. Green took possession late in the afternoon of Saturday, Sept. 16. His first public day in office was Monday, Sept. 18.

NOTORIETY OF MY ACTION.

The part I took in this life-and-death struggle with the "Ring," became completely and universally public by the newspapers of Sunday and Monday, Sept. 17 and 18. That at any time after those dates,—that at any time after Mr. Green was known to be in office,—that a week or ten days later,—Mr. Jennings could have said to me, what he professes to have said, in that interview, is impossible and absurd. I will show it to be so from the public journals.

THE TRIBUNE.

The Tribune of Monday morning, Sept. 18, which reached its readers many hours before Mr. Green could get into the Controller's office, had advised the public of the revolution which has taken place, and of the part in it which I had acted. It contained a leading editorial, from which the following is an extract :

Connolly refuses to resign, and *resolves to carry down in his own ruin* his late confederates. Samuel J. Tilden, Chairman of the Democratic State Committee, the adroitest and most far-seeing leader whom the death of Dean Richmond left to the Democracy of New York, *seizes the opportunity to use* Connolly for the *destruction* of the Ring, as the only salvation of the party. At his instance Connolly meets the demand for resignation that Hall might appoint his successor by virtually appointing his own successor. Andrew H. Green, to whom, as his Deputy, he makes over all the powers and duties of his office. Hall meets this check by assuming the power of removal he had declared, the day before, he did not possess, removing Connolly and appointing George B. McClellan in his place. Green is in possession by Connolly's legal appointment; McClellan is outside, awaiting possession, under Hall's appointment. The old leaders of the Democracy are coming forward to scourge Sweeney, Hall & Co. *back to their obscurity* in the ranks, and against them these members of *the broken* and *dissolving Ring* are in *open revolt.* That is the situation this morning.

It contained also another editorial headed, "Hall's Effort to Checkmate Tilden," and under a heading, "Mr. Tilden's Views," a half column report of an interview with me on Sunday. In that interview I am reported as saying that "the present state of the local Government would be made the subject of investigation and censure at the next Democratic State Convention;" that "*one* thing is *certain*, that the men who are the cause of all this corruption and demoralization would have to *go under*." The next morning, Sept. 19, *The Tribune* said :

Mr. Connolly is clearly right in the legal position, which, under the guidance of Mr. Tilden, he has assumed; Mr. Tilden deserves the sympathy of all good citizens, in so far as he is endeavoring to rid a great political party of a corrupt "Ring," that has well nigh ruined it and us.

THE TIMES.

The first notice in the *Times* of Mr. Green's being put in as Deputy, in name—a substitute in fact,—for Connolly, was on Sunday, Sept. 17, 1871. Look at the heading in the *Times* of that date, "Ruin of the Ring," in large capitals. Turn over to the editorial—double-leaded leader. It gives a flaming account of the transaction. It says: "The affair is being fought out in Democratic circles—honest Democrats against thieves." Now look at Monday's issue, Sept. 18. The capitals are larger than ever: "The Ring's Last Hope—Desperate Counter Movement of Mayor Hall—Possibility of violence being Resorted to by the Ring." In one of the columns a man is made to say, "I see the hand of Joab in this—I mean of Sam. Tilden." Turn to the double-leaded editorial,

The Ring at Bay.

Hall, Sweeny and Tweed are at length at bay, and they prepare to make one more desperate effort to keep the evidence of their guilt from the public eye. As we predicted yesterday, the action of Controller Connolly in removing his deputy, and designating Mr. Andrew H. Green as his successor, has *created* a PANIC in the Ring, as it forecasts nothing less than a full exposure of their guilt.

Look at Tuesday's (Sept. 19) issue. This contains Mr. O'Conor's opinion, in which he says: "My opinion on these two points has been requested by Mr. Tilden, Chairman of the Democratic State Committee." Notice the article headed, "A Day of Excitement:"

Towards the afternoon, Samuel J. Tilden arrived, and had a long interview with the Controller, and shortly afterwards it was given out that Mr. Charles O'Conor was preparing an opinion in support of the position the Controller had taken.

Again, in the article headed "Charles O'Conor's Opinion":

At the request of Mr. S. J. Tilden, Mr. Charles O'Conor yesterday gave the written opinion. * * * * Mr. Tilden, who has given the statutes a careful examination, fully concurs in Mr. O'Conor's view.

Again, under the heading "The Feeling in this City," the *Times* says:

The better-informed citizens, whose patriotic ardor prevented their working, *flocked* either to Mr. Tilden's house, in Gramercy Place, or to Gen. McClellan's office in the Department of Docks. Neither gentlemen was to be seen. Soon a rumor went round that Messrs. Tilden and O'Conor were preparing a legal exposition of the case in reply to the Mayor, and this comforted many.

THE WORLD.

On Wednesday, Sept. 20, *The World* contained an interview with Mr. Havemeyer, in which he stated my connection with the transaction. It contains the following:

Then I didn't see Connolly for three or four days. He promised to meet me at Samuel J. Tilden's last Friday night, but he didn't come, and I went to his house to hunt him up—I found him sick and almost ready to give way under the pressure. He said it was crucifying him. I put a little more backbone in him, and made him promise to come to Tilden's house at 10 o'clock next morning. He did so, and had his private counsel. Messrs. Beach and Courtney with him. Then Mr. Tilden had found that clause in the law about delegating all the authority to the Deputy-Controller in certain cases, and we advised Connolly to appoint Andrew H. Green his Deputy, and give him the general charge of the office. Connolly did so, and the whole thing was fixed up that day (Saturday) as clean as a whistle.

R.—What was your object in getting Mr. Green into the office ? Is it to assist the Committee of Seventy to make their investigation ? Mr. H.—Partly that. That is, to allow the Citizens' Committee that is acting with the Aldermen to make their investigation. That is all the investigation we want.

Meanwhile Mr. Marble had returned. *The World* of the 21st contained the following :

The only effective blows against Tammany in the recent excitement have been dealt by Democratic hands. Mr. Tilden is Chairman of the Democratic State Committee.

On the 22d *The World* said :

The astuteness of Mr. Tilden enabled him to strike a more staggering blow by pointing out to Mr. Connolly and his Democratic adviser the method by which the City Treasury had been wrenched from the control of the Tammany chiefs, and put under the guardianship of Mr. Green, another Democrat.

INTERVIEW.

The Brooklyn Eagle of Sept. 21, contained a long interview with me in which the whole controversy was discussed. In it I stated:

I told Mr. Connolly, when he first sought an interview with me, on last Friday, to ask my advice, that he might as well make up his mind that, as a political power, he and all others connected with the transactions which had excited the public indignation, *had ceased to exist.* My opinion is that the *fall* must *carry down* the *organization which these men control.* In other words, the Democratic party of this city and county must be *reorganized* by an EDICT of the *Democratic party of the State.*

This interview was copied into the *World* of the next morning.

EARLIER ACTION.

On the 15th, when visited by a *Times* reporter, I denied all connection with the movements for Connolly's resignation, and said : "I don't think the medicine is powerful enough for the disease."

Even earlier, on Sept. 11, when the time arrived for preparation for the State Convention, I issued a lithograph letter to 26,000 citizens, reaching every voting precinct outside of New York and Brooklyn. In it I said :

The league between corrupt Republicans and corrupt Democrats which was formed during Republican ascendency was too strong for honest men in 1870. The charter of that year had the votes of nearly all the Republicans. I denounced it in a public speech. Whenever the gangrene of corruption has reached the Democratic party we must take a knife and cut it out by the roots.

This, of course, soon got into the newspapers, from some one of the 26,000 correspondents. It is alluded to in *The Eagle* of the 21st, as *already familiar.* It was copied into the *Tribune* on the 22d, and into the *World* on the 23d.

The interview was on the following week. It was *after* a blow at the "Ring" had been struck which they—the newspapers—and all the public thought fatal to them. It was *after* it was universally known that I had, on a sudden emergency, planned and instantly executed that surprise. It was *after* a week of public contest on my part to hold the position—on the part of the "Ring" to recapture it. It was *after* the press had been full of the controversy for a *week* or *ten days*.

If anybody can be found to credit that *after* all this,—Mr. Jennings lectured and bullied me—to " let the public know " on *which side* I was *prepared* to fight—what " censure " would fall on me if I " *still refused* to *join* in the *attack* "—on my " *inaction* "—or that I " *begged* " that " the interview might be *kept secret;*" that in " a mournful undertone" I " *promised* to *put on* my armor *without delay ;*" that I was " afraid " of "my shadow ;" "appeared to think Tweed was waiting, etc., etc., let him come forward. Mr. Jennings himself will scarcely be that man.

The impossibility of this tissue of statements having one atom of truth appears by facts notorious, from the first day Mr. Green was in office.

There had been no interview, any time prior to the one about which this singular hallucination exists in Mr. Jennings' mind. I had not seen him for a long period. No such thing as he relates ever happened in any interview with me. That meeting was casual. I knew nothing of an interview being contemplated until Mr. Jennings himself proposed it to me, as I accidentally met him, seated with Mr. Jones, in Mr. Green's office, where I went with no more anticipation of meeting him, than I should have of his dreaming out such a tale of "imaginary conversations." Whose memory it is that has reached that last stage of infirmity in which it remembers what never happened, the public must judge from the records of notorious events which make it impossible that this narration should have in it any vestige of anything but fiction.

Mr. TILDEN, in his account of the interview which seems to have excited the resentment of the *Times*, did not impute to it any want of courage, energy or persistence in its warfare on the "Ring." In reply to its allegation that the battle was "over" when he joined it, he showed by this illustration that very long after he joined it, the *Times* did not consider the battle "over ;" that it seemed to feel—not unnaturally or discreditably—the strain of a long-continued controversy ; that help seemed to be desired and was welcomed ; and that even to the last, the battle was heavy and difficult. All this is true ; and to admit it or to assert it is no disparagement to the services of the *Times*.

The recent articles in which the *Times* began its many-column attack on Mr. TILDEN are full of the feeling of a desperate and anxious struggle, craving for more support than was received. The truth is that the almost universal sentiment of those engaged in the contest, even up to the day of the election, was not hopeful. It was a difficult and, in some respects, an unequal contest. In the last month of it Mr. TILDEN had become confident of a favorable result. The articles from the *Times*, cited below, show that, even then, it was not exempt from the general feeling of uneasiness. As late as the 15th of October, it said : "As yet *the fight is but beginning.*" On the 26th, twelve days before the election, it depicted in gloomy colors the public feeling. It said "*the same hopeless feeling was creeping over us as prevailed during the palmy days of the Ring.*"

STATEMENT OF THE "TIMES" THAT THE BATTLE WAS "OVER" WHEN MR. TILDEN ENTERED IT, REFUTED BY THE "TIMES."

Outlook of the Battle—ten weeks after Mr. Tilden's movement with Mr. Kernan—four weeks after Mr. Green's entry into the Comptrollership.

[*Times Editorial, October* 15, 1871.]

NO FALSE SECURITY.

The citizens of New York have so long neglected their own affairs, that it is hardly to be wondered at if they find it somewhat *irksome* to give them the *sustained* attention which is *absolutely necessary* now. The adversary is *sleeplessly active and watchful.* With the Ring it is simply a *question of life and death*, and, though working for the most part in the dark, they are *struggling* with all the *energy* of despair to defeat the popular demand for restitution and justice. An evening paper finds fault with the *Times* for refusing to believe that Tammany's power for evil *has departed.* That journal apparently supposes that much wishing and unlimited faith are all that is required to make the reformers masters of the situation. We shall believe that Tweed & Co. are dead, politically, when we see them in the State Prison. Until then, we shall hold it as treachery to the cause of reform to endeavor to lull people into security by hallooing that the enemy is routed. *As yet,* the *fight* is BUT BEGINNING. The Ring has the control of the ballot-box, and it can cheat the people out of their votes, let the strength of their opposition be what it may. The Ring has the District Attorney under its thumb ; the Corporation Counsel is its hired advocate, and it has the means of packing juries warranted to acquit city plunderers, whatever be the strength of the charges against them. The local Judges who can be trusted to act fearlessly and independently are the remarkable exceptions, instead of the rule. The Ring can fight the tax-payers through officers paid out of the public treasury, and can retain the services of thousands of men at the people's expense for the sole purpose of cheating the people out of their rights.

Against this what have the people gained ? A representative committee [Committee of Seventy] who are expected to attend to every abuse of local government at the same moment that they are, in the face of innumerable obstacles, fighting for the recovery of millions of plundered money ; an honest and upright man in the Controller's office [Andrew H. Green] who will see that not a dollar of public money is expended unless there is a valid and legal reason for it ; the unflinching support of a Judge [George G. Barnard !], all the vigor of whose character is now enlisted on the side of purity and justice.

Outlook of the Battle a Week Later.

[*Times Editorial, Oct.* 21, 1871.]

If the approaching election could be won by people sitting down at home or in their offices, and *wishing* for victory, there would be very little reason to doubt that TWEED's boasts about carrying the Tammany ticket by an overwhelming majority would come to grief. But good wishes, although better than nothing, will not suffice to overcome the enemy before us. There *must* be hard work done, and of that hard work *there is not quite so much promise at present as we should like to see*. It is probable that we must make up our minds to have one section of Republicans acting in pretty much the same way as they did last year.

* * * * * * *

Honest Democrats are *quite as anxious* to get rid of TWEED & Co. as any Republican can be. But the trouble is that honest men are not acting in harmony with each other. They do not know precisely how to go to work. They have to *oppose a compact organization*, and they are not only not much assisted, but are sometimes actually embarrassed by their own leaders. There is time enough, however, for all this muddle to be cleared up before election. The *spirit* is about to beat Tammany. All that is necessary is to bring it into shape and use it in a practical manner.

Outlook of the Battle a week later still.—Twelve days before the Election.

[*Times Editorial, Oct.* 26*th*, 1871.]

A blow is to be struck at last against the robbers of the City Treasury, and every honest man will agree that it is not a moment too soon. It is high time that New York should be relieved of the gross scandal of a man like the "Boss" buying his way into the State Senate with the money of the plundered tax-payers, and defying an outraged public to prevent him obtaining the means of robbing them still further. We have been told that prison bars could not save us from the colossal scoundrelism of TWEED; that the roughs, whom he holds at his beck, were stronger than the honest citizens of New York, and that, struggle as it might, the community could not unloose the grasp of ruffians from its throat, or force their hands out of its pocket. *The same* HOPELESS *feeling was creeping over us as prevailed during the palmy days of the Ring.* Then, no one doubted that they stole upon a scale which was absolutely without parallel, but they were so securely intrenched behind cunningly-devised laws, fraudulent voting machinery, and a whole army of accomplices, composed of influential capitalists as well as of loafers, prize-fighters, and convicted felons, that, with but *few exceptions*, people thought it an IMPOSSIBLE *enterprise to* DEFEAT *or even* DISTURB *them*. When the proofs of their guilt were made clear to all the world, and people were startled to find how much it has exceeded the most extravagant estimates, it seemed as if a wave of popular anger would at once sweep the whole infamous gang from place and power. But when, instead of being sent to pick oakum and break stones like other thieves, the Tammany Ring *continued to rule* us as heretofore, to *laugh at Courts* and *public opinion*, and even to extract sympathy from one or two weak-minded people, the *old exploded tradition* of their *wonderful resources* and *amazing strength of following* were *revived*, and a deeply wronged community *showed some sign of* GOING TO SLEEP AGAIN.

If *anything can* arouse the New York public to that pitch of indignation which alone becomes them in the present crisis, *it is the accounts* which we publish to-day. Here we have, thanks to the labors of Mr. SAMUEL J. TILDEN, *full* and *conclusive evidence* that WM. M. TWEED differs only from a common thief in having stolen tens of thousands instead of tens of dollars.

WHEN THE "BATTLE" REALLY BEGUN.

The first fallacy of the "*Times*" is in representing that the battle was "over" before it was really begun. The second fallacy is in representing that the battle was going on at a time long previous to the period when an election contest usually commences.

A week after the interview between Mr. TILDEN and Mr. KERNAN in Albany, at which a contest to crush the "Ring" was resolved upon, the "*Times*" had the following :

[*Times Editorial, August* 11, 1871.]

The Fall Election—What will the Anti-Tammany Democrats of the City do?

The time has already arrived for the *preliminary movements* of politicians in regard to the Fall election. According to the usual custom, the State Conventions of both parties should assemble early in September.

Three days earlier,—four days after Mr. TILDEN and Mr. KERNAN had arranged the preliminaries of the movement, ten days after the "*Times*" had finished its publication of the "Secret Accounts," the "*Times*" *first* addressed itself to the Democracy, as follows :

[*Times Editorial, August* 8, 1871.]

We should like to ask certain gentlemen, prominent in the Democratic party of this State, what they are going to do about the exposures which Tammany is now undergoing? We refer to such men as HORATIO SEYMOUR, SANFORD E. CHURCH, Justice ALLEN, FRANCIS KERNAN, and SAMUEL J. TILDEN. They are leaders in the Democratic Party. Their advice is looked for in any great emergency, and it has seldom been withheld. What have they to say now, when their associates in party leadership are under so dark a cloud?

Do they think they can afford to be silent, and let themselves and their party be involved in the disgrace that has been brought home to Tammany? Up to this time Tammany alone has been attacked. We have not endeavored to hold the party responsible for the offenses of our city rulers. We have expressly said, over and over again, that the questions at issue were not of a party character, but turned upon *facts ;* and upon them we have appealed to Democrats, as well as Republicans, for a verdict.

* * * * * * *

PERIOD BEFORE THE BATTLE.

Even in the previous period, it is not true that Mr. Tilden's position was unknown. There was *no* time when it was doubtful. There was no moment when the *Times* itself doubted what that position was.

In its present industrious detraction, it admits :

"We never questioned the fact that Mr. Tilden, all this time, in his heart detested the Tammany gang, but he took care never to say so," etc., etc.

The truth is, he never made or accepted any new relations, after a long series of open contests; he never hesitated to oppose the "Ring." That the *Times* knew this, is proved by a few specimen extracts, which are appended.

[*Times, May 13th*, 1871.]

Views of Eminent American Jurists.

After reading the letters from Samuel J. Tilden, Esq., A. C. Hand, Esq., and Judge Edmonds—which are appended—Mr. Evarts proceeded with his argument.

[*Times Editorial, May 13th*, 1871.]

The Bill for Gagging the Press and the Public.

Mr. Samuel J. Tilden is among the numerous Democratic lawyers who regard the amendments passed under the lash of Tweed and Sweeney as an outrage upon the people.

* * * * * * *

At the very moment when a Committee of the Bar of this city was before the Governor, calling his attention to their outrageous provisions, and Democratic lawyers, like Samuel J. Tilden, join in the protests, the editor of the *Express* says, "we have not seen them."

[*Times Editorial, August 17th*, 1871.]

There were a few indignant protests against the scheme [Charter of 1870] uttered by such high-toned Democrats as Samuel J. Tilden and others of his character ; but they were without effect, for Tweed and Sweeney had the votes already bought up. Of all the Republican Senators, Senator Thayer alone is on record as voting against it.

[*Times Editorial, October 6*, 1871.]

There would be no doubt where a gentleman of Mr. SAMUEL TILDEN's character would be found in such a contest as this.

First Popular Meeting, Sept. 4, 1871, at which Committee of Seventy were appointed—and afterwards.

[*Times Editorial, September 6th*, 1871.]

"If," says the *World*, "Mr. Astor, or Mr. Stewart, or Mr. Belmont, or Mr. Barlow had been chairman of the meeting, and the list of speakers had comprised such names as General Dix, Mr. O'Conor, Mr. Greeley, Mr. Tilden, Mr. Bryant, Marshall O. Roberts and Judge Blatchford, the meeting might have been deemed to be an expression of the best public opinion of the city." All these gentlemen, however, as the *World* says, "stood aloof," and it tries to give the impression that they discountenanced the meeting. We do not know how the gentlemen named will like to be thus represented as allies of the Ring ; but if we are not mistaken, *every one* of them, with the *possible exception* of Messrs. Astor, O'Conor and Roberts, *heartily sympathised* with the meeting, and several of them wrote letters to the Committee of Arrangements regretting their inability to attend.

[*Times Editorial, Sept.* 5, 1871.]

" An article published in another column shows the views that were entertained of the Charter by such Democrats as Samuel J. Tilden,

*   *   *   *   *   *   *

and we have no doubt the same views are now entertained by ALL *honest* Democrats throughout the State. The first thing which the next Legislature should do, therefore, is to repeal the Charter, and restore to the people the right of self-government that has been usurped by the Tammany oligarchy."

[*Times, Sept.* 5th, 1871.]

" We give an extract from the speech of the nominal head of the Democratic party of this State, Samuel J. Tilden, made on the 4th day of April, 1870, before the Charter was passed ; and in an effort to try to prevent the passage of so undemocratic a measure."

[*Times, Sept.* 18, 1871.]

" At the St. Nicholas, and the Grand, and the Grand Central, the St. James, and Hoffman House, Mr. Connolly's action was canvassed under every possible light, and was considered wonderfully shrewd. In fact, at the Grand Central, a gentleman who looked like a rural Democrat, of good position, blurted out, " Gentlemen, don't deceive yourselves, Connolly never did this on his own head. I see the hand of Joab in this; I mean of Sam. Tilden. And I'll tell you what it is, the good old days of the Democracy are going to be revived, and Havemeyer, Andrew Green, Sam. Tilden, and the good old leaders are going to purge the party of its ruffians."

[*Times Editorial, Nov.* 2, 1871.]

If the people will not believe Republicans, surely they will find it hard to refute the evidence of Democrats like CHARLES O'CONOR and SAMUEL J. TILDEN.

[*Times Editorial, Nov.* 2, 1871.]

The appearance on the same platform of SAMUEL J. TILDEN and WM. M. EVARTS, and GEN. SIGEL, and Gov. SEYMOUR, is a significant evidence of a new era in Municipal politics, and should convince every honest man that the issues before us in the present election are above the region of party strife, and rest upon principles higher and more essential than those in dispute between Republicans and Democrats.

[*Times Editorial, Oct.* 29, 1871.]

The nomination of such men as HORATIO SEYMOUR in the Assembly District, misrepresented by the notorious TOM FIELDS, and the acceptance by SAMUEL J. TILDEN of a similar nomination in obedience to dictates of the most enlightened public spirit, are therefore encouraging symptoms for the future.

These are but specimens—a few out of many.

THE ELECTION OF 1868.

[*Times, Editorial, February* 10, 1873.]

And while Mr. TILDEN is about it, will he explain to the public how he, in company with WM. M. TWEED, swindled the people and stuffed the ballot-boxes in 1868, so that it was made to appear that SEYMOUR and HOFFMAN carried this State over GRANT and GRISWOLD? No one knows better than SAMUEL J. TILDEN what a farce and a fraud that election was, and Mr. TILDEN knows just as well that it was in his power to have given the people a fair election.   *   *   *   *

Mr. TILDEN was TWEED'S partner in the shameless trickery of 1868.

It is scarcely necessary to reply that there is not a particle of truth in any of these statements. They are total fictions.

Nobody ever pretended, as a matter of fact, that Mr. Tilden had any knowledge of, agency in, or gave any aid or countenance to any frauds, in that or any other election. Nobody could so pretend without utter falsehood.

In the winter of 1868–9 a Congressional Committee made an elaborate and protracted investigation into the alleged frauds at the then recent election. The evidence, incidentally developed—for nobody professed to charge, or even suspect, any complicity on the part of Mr. Tilden—showed facts and relations which proved the contrary.

The argument, or inference, that he must have acquired knowledge of such frauds as Chairman of the State Committee, or had power to prevent them, is without any foundation. What were the relations between Mr. Tilden and the men accused of those frauds and receiving the benefit of them, and where the power to prevent such frauds really resided will now be shown.

As stated on page 13 of the letter, in the passage respecting the "formative period" of the "Ring," the antagonism between those who became its leading members, and Mr. Tilden was "sharply defined and public." This antagonism had begun as early as 1863.

In the State Convention of September, 1868, there was an open contest. Mr. ALLEN C. BEACH was nominated,—chiefly by the efforts of Mr. Tilden—for Lieutenant-Governor by a large majority. The result was described in the *Times* as a triumph over Tammany. In August, an elaborate attack on Mr. Tilden by one of the journals of the "Ring" was copied into the *Leader*, edited by Mayor Hall.

Mr. Tilden was about the last man in the State to whom these persons would have entrusted any of their secrets or plans. Still less would they expose to him any illegal or fraudulent schemes of theirs.

The State Committee had no function in respect to the conduct of the election in this city. Mr. Tilden did not belong to the General Committee of the city, and during the years of the ascendancy of the "Ring" in the city organizations, had no connection with those organizations—no voice in local nominations—and never asked or accepted any appointment for a friend. At that time, he had about as much relation to the ruling powers of Tammany as Mayor Havemeyer may be supposed to have to the clique now controlling the local Republican organization, whom he has lately described with so much picturesque effect.

The State Committee was an object of jealousy and fear to these men. It was at all times perfectly independent of them, and received very little aid in contributions towards its moderate and necessary expenses—and often none—from the whole office-holding class of the city.

In the election of 1868, the "Ring" were playing their own personal game. Even in 1864, it had been suspected that the leading persons who afterwards formed the "Ring," were untrue to HORATIO SEYMOUR, the Democratic candidate for Governor, as well as to GEN. MCCLELLAN. They never forgave Gov. Seymour for vetoing the Broadway Railroad Bill, in 1863, in which they, with their Republican allies, had become largely interested.

In 1868, it was believed before the election that they had plotted a scheme to keep HORATIO SEYMOUR, the Democratic candidate for President, behind his ticket. They did, in fact, withhold from him all the votes they could without detection, and bargained with the corrupt Republicans with whom they were in partnership, at his expense. Their constant study was to pervert to their own selfish gain the efforts and sacrifices of four millions of Democratic voters in the country, and four hundred and fifty thousand in this State. They never hesitated to sacrifice or to sell the general objects of the Democratic party, its principles or its measures. They never contributed to its advancement, except so far as was necessarily incidental to their own purposes of holding power in the Municipal Government.

Their object Mr. Tilden never had any sympathy with, or any disposition to promote. At the time of the election in 1868, the Presidential contest had already been lost in the October elections; and he had only to fulfil his duty towards the Democracy of the State and Union. It appeared in the Congressional investigations, that not only did he have no connection with the naturalizations, but he did not even know who were the naturalization committee of either party, or where they had their offices. The first fruit of the success of the "Ring" in gaining increased influence at Albany, by that election, was a scheme immediately concocted to depose Mr. Tilden from the State Committee.

The power of the "Ring" in this city had been derived from Republican Legislation, and the corrupt means by which they had obtained that Legislation, were a division of the city offices, contracts, jobs and bribery. In 1868, and for three years previous, the Mayor, Comptroller and Street Commissioner were removable by the Governor; half the Supervisors were Republicans, and nearly all the Commissions, embracing vast patronage, were Republican.

The Inspectors of Election—the Canvassers who counted the votes—the Clerks of the Polls—and the Registers were all appointed by the Board of Police Commissioners. Half of the members of this Board and all its chief officers were Republicans. Thomas C. Acton was its President; Seth C. Hawley its Chief Clerk; S. C. Hawley, Jr., Secretary; and John A. Kennedy, Superintendent of Police.

It would have been impossible to credit beforehand that, under these circumstances, at a hotly contested Presidential election, when the Republican party was watchful, and straining itself to the utmost—systematic frauds in voting and canvassing could be perpetrated without the complicity of the leading representatives of the Republican party in the city; nor is it easy now to see how that was possible.

The idea of imputing to Mr. Tilden responsibility for election frauds, of which he had no knowledge beforehand, with which he was in no manner connected—and which he in no wise aided or abetted—on the assumption that "it was in his power to have given the people a fair election," when he had had no voice in shaping the Election Laws or appointing the Election Officers—which laws had been made by the Republicans, and which officers were practically appointed by the Republicans—is too absurd to need discussion.

The Assembly chosen at that election was, by a large majority, Republican. The Senate was Republican. It was in their power to alter the election laws, and the mode of appointing officers of the election. They did not. At the next session, when there was a Democratic majority, Mr. Tilden endeavored to do so; but *his* Election law was beaten, and the Election law under which Mayor Hall got the practical control of all these officers passed,—every Republican senator voting for it, and the *Times* filling the air with its laudations. The one element of good which that law contained—"watchers" of the canvass, to be appointed by the candidates, was taken from Mr. Tilden's bill.

The truth is, that frauds at elections are usually the work of men having a special, and often a pecuniary interest in the local results. Fanatics who commit crimes to advance their abstract ideas of National or State politics, are rare exceptions to the ordinary course of human nature. If a "Ring" had not already been formed—embracing the wire-workers of both party machines—such frauds as are alledged of the election of 1868 could not have been possible.

"TIMES" DENIAL THAT MR. TILDEN FURNISHED PROOFS, REFUTED BY THE "TIMES" ITSELF.

[*Times Editorial, Oct.* 26, 1871.]

Here we have, [Broadway Bank investigations], thanks to the labors of Mr. Samuel J. Tilden, *full* and *complete* EVIDENCE that Wm. M. Tweed differs only from a common thief in having stolen tens of thousands instead of tens of dollars.

[*Times Editorial, Oct.* 27, 1871.]

A million dollars out of the three millions and a-half of plunder that was deposited in the hands of E. A. WOODWARD, the distributing agent of the " Ring," has been TRACED *directly* to the *pockets* of TWEED.

[*Times Editorial, November* 2, 1871.]

The web of evidence woven around WILLIAM M. TWEED by the publication of the deposit and drawing accounts of INGERSOLL, GARVEY and E. A. WOODWARD, in connection with warrants from the Controller's Office, in the National Broadway Bank, and also certain deposit entries made in the name of TWEED, in the same bank, gives that gentleman no possible loophole for escape. He is like a stranded whale ; he can only flounder for a while.

CHARACTER OF THE CHARTER OF 1870.

[*Times Editorial, June* 1, 1871.]

Mayor Hall, a few weeks previous to his last election, chose some thirty men to govern the City of New York, among whom were Mr. Tweed for a term of *four* years, Mr. Sweeny and Mr. Connolly for *five* years, the Police Commissioners for from *five* to *eight* years, and the others mostly for *five* years. Does the *Post* regard his election immediately after as a verdict by the people approving these appointments? If the people had not so approved, and had turned him out, what *good would it have done them? What good would it do them* even to turn him out *at the next election?* Would they be any the *less* in the grip of the hungry thieves he has set to feed upon us, and to whom the Legislature, *as far as it can, has given us over for the next four years?*

[*Times Editorial, Sept.* 5, 1871.]

Repeal the Ring Charter.

It is obvious to every one who has thought over the present situation of the city, that the only mode of escape from the clutches of Hall and his colleagues lies in the total repeal of the Charter of 1870, with its subsequent amendments. That Charter was the exclusive invention of the " Ring," *and was a* FRAUD *from the beginning.* It was designed to *consolidate* and *perpetuate* ALL municipal power in the hands of an oligarchy of four men.

The Charter was passed April 5th, 1870.

[*Times Editorial, April 6, 1870.*]

Municipal Reform.

The almost *unanimous demand* of the people of this metropolis *for a thorough reform* in the election of officers, as well as in the general administration of affairs, *has been acceded to in a way and with a* celerity *which is remarkable.* Despite the incredulity as to the possibility of reform expressed by those who thought the city hopelessly given over to the control of lawlessness and corruption, *the voice of the law-abiding, order-loving, tax-paying class has been heeded.*

*　　*　　*　　*　　*　　*　　*

The new Charter received the vote of every Senator but two.

The new Charter is very generally conceded to be a good one. The vote by which it was passed ought certainly to be accepted as a sufficient guarantee that it is.

*　　*　　*　　*　　*　　*　　*

We have the assurance of the best men of both parties that *it is a substantial and reliable reform,* and from the examination we have been able to give it *we are inclined to concur in that opinion.* At all events, it is a vast improvement upon the old one, and if it shall be put in operation by Mayor Hall with that regard for the general welfare which we have reason to anticipate, we feel sure that our citizens will have reason to count *yesterday's work in the Legislature as most important and salutary.*

[*Times, April 13, 1870.*]

The good work goes on! A *new Charter,* an effective election law—and now the Board of Supervisors, with all its iniquities, is legislated out of existence. The *Tribune,* in its anxiety to comfort its exemplary friends of the Young Democracy, may see in these things only the handiwork of Satan. *But the citizens, who desire above all things good city government, note with pleasure the changes in progress, and are hopeful.*

[*Times Editorial, April 7, 1870.*]

The New Election Law.

The remarkable unanimity of sentiment in approval of the Election Law, which we gave in full yesterday, is *fully justified* by a CAREFUL EXAMINATION of its provisions. From *beginning* to *end*, it seems to have been *conceived in the true* interests of the people, and with an intention of enabling them to secure an honest expression of political sentiment and personal preferences. Of course it would be impossible in brief space to give the law a close analysis, or even to point out *seriatim* the changes which it makes. That is a work we must leave for the interested reader to do for himself at deliberate intervals, contenting ourselves with general comment.

*　　*　　*　　*　　*　　*　　*

We feel justified in *congratulating* the friends of law and order upon the enactment of this new law, as well as upon the hopeful assurance which it gives that *hereafter* the sources of our political action will be at least comparatively pure and undefiled, and that there is at least a *well-founded hope of deliverance* from the CORRUPTIONS which have so long pervaded our municipal administration.

CHARACTER OF THE APPOINTMENTS UNDER THE CHARTER OF 1870.

[*Times Editorial, August* 13, 1871.]

If, when the new charter went into effect, Mayor Hall had appointed as heads of the leading departments new men, who had been in no way identified with PREVIOUS FRAUDS, and if he had at the same time made a public exposure of the rascalities that had been perpetrated under the old charter, there would have been *some* REASON to *believe* that he and those with whom he acted *desired* and *intended* to bring about a reform in the city government. But he did *nothing* of the *kind*. On the contrary, he *selected* the *very men* who had been the *most* NOTORIOUS PLUNDERERS of the treasury—men whom the *World*, at the time they were appointed, was branding as "thieves and swindlers"—and placed them in the most *responsible positions under the new charter*. They were the men who framed the new charter and procured its passage through the Legislature ; and they framed it in such a way as to put the *whole power* of the municipal government in their own hands, and *increased* their *facilities* for *plunder* FAR BEYOND anything known under the *old* charter. Tweed was appointed to the head of the Department of Public Works ; Sweeny to that of Public Parks ; his brother-in-law to the position of Chamberlain, which Sweeny had left ; while all the other departments, with the possible exception of the Dock Commissioner, were filled with Tweed and Sweeny's tools and retainers a large portion of them being selected from the list of assemblymen who had helped them to lobby the charter through the Legislature.

The appointments of Mayor Hall, under the Charter of 1870, were made April 9th. A list of them appeared in the *Times* of April 11th.

On the same day, April 11th, Mr. OTTENDORFER denounced these appointments in the *Staats Zeitung*.

He characterised TWEED as "the very *soul* of the corruption of Tammany Hall." He asked, how can the Mayor justify himself for placing Tweed in "the Consolidated Street and Croton Department."

This article is quoted in the TIMES of September 7, 1871, as follows, from the "*Staats Zeitung*, the great and influential organ of the German Democracy."

[*From the Staats Zeitung, April* 11*th,* 1870.]

The Mayor attempts to justify the retention of Republicans who have hitherto been members of State Commissions, by saying that the support of the Charter by Republican members of the Legislature, and the character of the acting Boards demanded such action. Most certainly these reasons would demand the appointment of Republicans, but not of THESE Republicans. Among those retained there are men whose removal was as earnestly desired by the better sort of Republicans as by Democrats. Notably the Republicans retained in subordinate positions are the very men who are accused of being hand in glove with the Tammany Ring. What, for instance, will the long and bitter complaints against the Police Commission and the Department for the Survey of New Buildings amount to if those matters are left in just the hands which have hitherto controlled them ?

How *can* the Mayor *justify* himself, now that he has placed the *Consolidated Street* and *Croton Departments* in the *control* of a man who is the *very* SOUL of the CORRUPTION of Tammany Hall?

[*Times, April* 13, 1870.]

Our New City Government.

* * * * * * * *

From beginning to end *the Tweed party has not manifested the slightest disposition to evade or prevaricate.*

* * * * * * * *

It remains, now, to canvass the merits of the other appointments, and to do it in a fair and unpartisan spirit.

Before doing so, however, we feel justified in utterly disclaiming *any* OBLIGATION upon the part of the *Republican* party for the appointment of a minority of the several Commissioners from its ranks, and in denying to Mayor HALL any credit therefor. *The passage of the new charter and of the election law*,—the latter by far the more substantial reform of the two,—*could* NOT have been secured WITHOUT the help of the Republicans in the Legislature, and hence the credit is as much theirs as it is that of the TWEED Democracy.

* * * * * * *

As a whole, the appointments of the heads of the various departments of the City Government, which have been announced by the Mayor, are *far above the average* in point of personal fitness, and *should be satisfactory*. Many of them are excellent, some are bad, and others really offensive; still the good are in a large majority, and so distributed that, with a single exception, they can nullify and control the others. Considering the partisan obligations to be recognized, and the diverse interests to be conciliated and kept in harmony, *we feel inclined to be* THANKFUL, if not entirely satisfied with the result.

Beyond these general remarks, we cannot proceed with propriety or pleasure to make any personal mention, further than to record our very decided protest against the *personnel* of the Excise Commission.

The objection was *not* to TWEED or SWEENY, or to any but the most inconsiderable of their followers.

Laudations of Tweed.

[*Times, April* 8, 1870.]

Senator Tweed is in a fair way to distinguish himself as a reformer. Having gone so far as the champion of the new election bill and charter, he seems to have no idea of turning back. Perhaps, like Macbeth, he thinks that under existing circumstances "returning were as tedious as go o'er," but at all events *he has put the people of Manhattan Island under great obligations.* His last proposition to abolish the Board of Supervisors of New York and transfer their functions to the Mayor, Recorder, and new Board of Aldermen is the crowning act of all. It strikes a blow at one of the most corrupt departments of our Government, and one which is as useless as a fifth wheel to a coach. *We trust that Senator Tweed will manifest the same energy in the advocacy of this last reform which marked his action in regard to the charter."*

Confidence of the Republicans in Tweed.

[*Times Editorial,* May 1, 1870.]

* * * * * * * * *

The selection of Mr. Tracy for that position by the Board of Public Works has an added significance in the *comfortable assurance* which it affords to the tax-payers of our City that the MUNICIPAL REGIME now being ESTABLISHED will be in the general interest, and that the policy of the Board of Works, *under* Mr. TWEED'S *directions,* will be strictly in accord with the assurances which were given when the new Charter was adopted. It is evident that the Democratic leaders who have been *entrusted* with the *control* of the City Government are *disposed to act in good faith,* and that the *confidence* which was *bestowed upon them* by the REPUBLICANS in the Legislature, as well as by our best citizens, was not misplaced.

Confidence of the Republicans in A. Oakey Hall.

[*Times Editorial,* April 10, 1870.]

It is seldom that so high a *personal compliment* is paid to a public officer as was involved to him by the *passage* of the *new Charter.* We trust that he duly appreciates it, and that he WILL *act* in a manner to *justify* it. There were those who hesitated at placing such great powers in his hands—powers which were fraught with *permanent results for good or evil* to the *municipality;* but it was finally concluded that HE *was worthy* of the trust. REPUBLICANS and Democrats alike testified in his behalf, and have *practically put in* HIS keeping the FUTURE of the City for a *series of years.* Under such circumstances Mayor HALL cannot do otherwise than respond favorably to the general expectation and confidence so flatteringly extended to him. He *must,* and WE have NO DOUBT he *will,* appoint the VERY BEST *men* whose services can be secured to the heads of the various departments.

[*Times Editorial,* May 8, 1870.]

Whether the Mayor proposed it or not, he certainly approves the idea of having music in the parks for the benefit of the people who cannot afford to spend much money in amusements. * * *

The Mayor and his friends will deserve the thanks of the public if they persevere with the design, in spite of all objections.

[*Times Editorial,* June 7th, 1870.]

* * * * * * *

Upon the result of its action the success of the new experiment very largely depends, and it is to be hoped that the members will address themselves to the work before them *in a spirit of wise reform, and with an unpartisan regard for the general good. The Mayor's message, at any rate, shows them the road they ought to pursue.*

THE CHARTER OBTAINED by *buying* REPUBLICANS and *against* SAMUEL J. TILDEN.

[*Times Editorial,* August 17, 1871.]

"The recent revelations respecting the finances of our city, show how NECESSARY it seemed to the Tammany leaders to find some pretext for legislation which would *perpetuate their control of the affairs* of the city government, not only as against the Republicans *but against the Democrats, among whom existed a wide spread discontent.* The awfullest tyranny of the politicians who controlled Tammany Hall, had already *consolidated* an *opposition*, which had the POWER to OVERTHROW them, and this opposition manifested itself immediately upon the assembling of the Legislature of 1870. The cry of a new charter was started in the expectation that one might be passed which would prolong the tenure of Tammany's power. A charter was proposed by the Tammany men; but the Young Democracy at once dispelled these fond hopes by defeating it. It was then that Sweeney, true to his cowardly instincts, took himself away from Albany in confusion and fright, leaving general dismay in his rear. Soon, however, the idea of BUYING a charter THROUGH got possession of the mind of the magnates, and *negotiations* were *promptly set on foot. There were a few indignant protests against the scheme uttered by such* HIGH-TONED Democrats as SAMUEL J. TILDEN *and* others of his character ; but they were without effect, *for Tweed* and *Sweeney had the voters already* BOUGHT *up.* Of ALL the *Republican Senators*, Senator Thayer ALONE, is on record as voting against it.

Two days before the passage of the Charter of April 5th, 1870, the defeat of the Charter which gave Spring elections—no appointments till *after* a new election—and created full responsibility to the people was thus described. The defeat of this Charter and the passage of the other were part of the same scheme.

[*Times Editorial, April* 3, 1870.]

The Victory of the Ring.

* * * * * * * * *

A great battle has lately been fought at Albany. It was known far and wide that such a battle was to be fought. The confidence of the leaders of one army was so sanguine and so freely expressed, that a considerable part of the community seemed to believe in their anticipated victory. Opinion, at least, was pretty fairly divided, much as it used to be in New York, over the first day's news of a general engagement between the Union and Confederate armies. The news of a result exactly opposite to that so buoyantly prognosticated, was so stunning in some quarters as the news of Austerlitz was to PITT. Numbers thereafter went about asking how it happened that clever men—for among the heads of the "Young Democracy" there are clever men—could have been so egregiously deceived. Yet the answer is very simple. There was *something to be bought*, and there was PLENTY of MONEY to BUY it. All that was needed besides, was plenty of nerve, and plenty of shrewdness, and the "Ring" has never shown itself deficient in either of these desiderants.

* * * * * * * * *

By habits and education, the strong men of the "Ring" work habitually in that way. They are sagacious, energetic, and manifestly *believe* they are *justified* in the adoption of EXTRAORDINARY MEANS to *gain* the end of a PROTRACTED TENURE of *power*. With such oligarchs as these in office, strongly banded together and possessed of almost limitless wealth, it is not easy to see what machinery of popular government could be devised that they might not go behind to run it for their own purposes. * * * * * * * *

[*Times, April* 13, 1870.]

* * * * * * * * *

The passage of the new charter and of the Election law, the latter by far the more substantial reform of the two—could NOT have been secured WITHOUT the help of the Republicans in the Legislature, and HENCE THE CREDIT IS AS MUCH THEIRS as it is that of the TWEED Democracy.

* * * * * * * * *

[*Times* Editorial, *April* 6*th.*]

One of the most singular things connected with the whole affair seems to us to be the entire lack of influence exerted by the Union League Club, or by Mr. Greeley, as their accredited spokesman, even upon the Republican members of the Legislature. It would have been fair to expect that so pronounced an expression by that body would have been headed by at least one Republican Senator, but it seems that it was not.

[*Times Editorial, April* 12, 1870.]

Checkmate in two Moves.

* * * * * * * *

While Mr. Greeley was thus flirting with Morrissey and O'Brien, the Union League Club—which a great authority has told us consists of a "narrow-minded set of blockheads"—deputed him to go to Albany to protest against the charter as it then stood. Mr. Greeley went, and very opposite accounts have been given of his doings at the capital. His course seems to have been a little wild. Like other persons given to flirting, first he would, and then he wouldn't. The result was, that between two stools he came to the ground. He did the Tweed party no harm, and the narrow-minded set of blockheads no good. There was no one left to comfort the great political economist; he was left forsaken, even by Mr. Samuel Tilden—like Dido deserted Æneas. Short, indeed, has been the new alliance—like the baby mentioned in the epitaph, one wonders what on earth it was begun for. Presently we shall see another long letter addressed to "Samuel Tilden, Esq.," informing him that he is also no better than one of the wicked.

* * * * * *

The Union League Club thought they could do as they pleased with the players on each side, but like the traditional "Three Tailors of Tooley street," they are left gazing at the stars on their backs. The rebellious Democrats are receiving baskets of saw-dust, one after the other. Of their successors we shall have more to say to-morrow. At present we only hint to the victorious section—no opportunity lasts long which is not used wisely. Mr. TWEED *and his friends* are not so POOR *but* they could *manage to exist* under a purer form of Government than we have seen of late years in the city.

The Mayor's proclamation was probably suggested, at least in part, by his well-known propensity to "poke fun" at the company which he happens to be addressing. He begins by telling the Republicans that but for his own incurable good nature, he might have driven them all forth into the hungry world without a crust. "He would be politically justified" in conferring "every one of the thirty-two appointments upon Democrats." But he is merciful, and will give some of the crumbs that fall from the table to the Republicans.

Let us be thankful—only we have a vague idea that the Republicans were rather useful to the authors of the new charter in the recent contest. But for the Republicans, the Young Democracy might to-day be at the top of the tree, and the grand sachems hanging all of a row to the lower branches. But the Mayor is not serious. He must have his joke. Mr. Hall and his associates will doubtless show a proper appreciation of the assistance rendered them by the Republicans when the enemy was crying, "War to the knife, and the knife to the hilt."

Jeering of the Ring's Enemies.

(*Times*, April 19, 1870.)

Now is the triumph of Tweed complete! In the innermost recesses of Tammany the two factions met last night in mortal conflict—and the representatives of the Young Democracy were left upon the ground, helpless and humiliated. At the annual meeting for the election of officers, two tickets were presented—one beginning with Mr. Oakey Hall and ending with Mr. Sweeny; the other embracing Messrs. Fox, Tilden, Morrissey, Marble, A. H. Green, and other heroes of the O'Brien faction.

[*Times Editorial, August*, 17, 1871.]

The Central Park, and How it Fell into the Hands of the Ring.

It was for a long time doubted whether it could be possible that the Senate would ever consent to put the Central Park under the control of the City Ring. Public meetings exclaimed against such an outrage, and a large deputation of influential citizens was sent to Albany to bear the people's protest. Arriving at Albany, these gentlemen received from TWEED and SWEENY, full assurances that the Park Commission should be retained under the new charter, and that no essential change should be made in its *personnel*. MR. NATHANIEL SANDS was prolific of the promises in the same direction. There seemed to be no one really in favor of touching the Park Commissioners. But it subsequently appeared Mr. TOM. FIELDS, Mr. HENRY HILTON, and Mr. PETER B. SWEENY, were the chief agents in foisting this obnoxious feature into the charter.

* * * * * * *

And by this precious trio was perpetrated this OUTRAGEOUS act, which INSULTED *public sentiment*, by interfering with and partially *destroying* the Central Park Commission, whose record was unstained, and whose noble services were appreciated by every man, woman, and child in New York. * * * * * *

The charter passed. It gave A. OAKEY HALL the appointment of about forty heads of Departments, and, among them, of five members of the Department of Parks. *Only about ten days more official life was given to the Park* Commissioners, and then they *ceased to be*. The new Department of Parks made its entry upon the stage, and took possession of a work for which its members were UTTERLY *unfitted*, as will be shown with reasonable clearness when we come to consider *who* they were, and *by whom* they were appointed.

Confidence in Sweeny.

[*Times, May* 21, 1870.]

Central Park.

Yesterday the Commissioners of Public Parks held a meeting, Mr. Peter B. Sweeny presiding. Nothing was done which tends to justify the apprehensions of those who looked upon a change in the old Commission as a sure precursor of an era of chaos and jobbery. Mr. Sweeny has distinctly *pledged* himself not to permit *any tampering* with a property which the public values above all its other possessions. *That he will be faithful to his word* the meeting yesterday afforded a *fresh guarantee*.

The "Ring" Sham of a "Reform" Common Council— Patronized.

[*Times Editorial, May* 3, 1870.]

THE ALDERMANIC TICKET.

We trust that Mayor HALL and his coadjutors, in the preparation of the ticket to be presented to our citizens at the forthcoming election of Aldermen, will not forget the pledges given when the new charter was under consideration at Albany.

*   *   *   *   *   *   *   *   *   *

If the promoters of the new charter are prepared to act fairly—if they desire to make effective the reform implied in the abolition of the old Board of Aldermen—they will discard weak and worthless names, whatever their professed political affiliations, and will give to the city a list which shall at once furnish a guarantee of upright local government, and redeem the promise with which Messrs. TWEED and HALL rescued the charter from jeopardy.

[*Times Editorial, May* 19, 1870.]

MUNICIPAL POLITICS.

The public apathy about political affairs which exists in this City is undoubtedly caused in a great degree, by the unwillingness of respectable men to fill municipal offices. The Democrats, *to do them justice*, made an EFFORT *to put respectable names* on their Aldermanic ticket, but the merchants and bankers, whom they nominated, and in whose hands everybody acknowledges the municipal interests would be perfectly safe— at least as far as their power went—refused to serve, and we were accordingly furnished with a second edition, made up of the same old party hacks from whose rule we have already suffered so much.

These extracts prove:

1st. That at the time the Charter of 1870 was passed, the *Times* knew its nature, objects and effect ; knew that it operated to put Tweed, Hall and Sweeny in supreme dominion over the people of this city for a series of years, without any power to remove them, without any power in the people, at an election, to change the system or the men.

2nd. That the *Times* not only knew beforehand that Tweed, Hall and Sweeney were to be made dictators of the city for a long series of years by the Charter of 1870, but after the appointments had been made, it approved them. It continued from day to day, during the Summer, its plaudits of Tweed, Hall and Sweeney, and never intimated discontent with them till September 20th, and then chiefly employed itself in attacking their Democratic adversaries.

During this period, the greatest frauds which have been since disclosed, were perpetrated.

3rd. That at the time the Charter passed, the *Times* knew the corrupt means by which it was carried.

One of these means, was a division of offices, agreed upon, before the vote, between the "Ring" and corrupt Republicans. These agreements the *Times* avowed. It claimed the fulfilment of them. It asserted that the Charter could not have passed without the aid of the Republicans. It said: "Mr. Hall and *his* ASSOCIATES will doubtless show a proper appreciation of the assistance rendered them by the Republicans." It commended the "Ring" for keeping its bargain, saying, four days after the division of offices had been carried into effect, "the Tweed party has not manifested the slightest disposition to evade or prevaricate."

The other means was the BUYING of the Republican Senators and Assemblymen with MONEY.

This also the *Times* knew before the passage of the Charter. It said, April 3d, "There was something *to be* BOUGHT and plenty of MONEY to BUY it.

It said afterwards (Aug. 17th, 1871), "Tweed and Sweeney had the votes already bought up. Of ALL the Republican Senators, Senator Thayer *alone* is on record voting against it."

4th. That the *Times* knew, when the Charter passed, it

could not be done without a large support of the Republicans, and against the resistance and protest of Mr. Tilden and other Democrats.

It asserted (April 12th, 1870), that "but for the Republicans" the Tweed Democracy might have been beaten by Democratic resistance.

It claimed (April 13th, 1870) that the Charter "could *not* have been secured *without the help* of the Republicans in the Legislature, and hence the credit is as much *theirs* as it is that of the Tweed Democracy."

It declared the year after (August 17th, 1871), that "the tyranny of Tammany Hall had already consolidated an opposition which had the POWER to overthrow them," when the "idea of BUYING a Charter THROUGH got possession of the minds of the magnates, and negotiations were promptly set on foot."

It helped to carry the Charter over the Union League, the *Tribune*, the *World*, the *Evening Post* and the *Sun*, and against the open opposition of Mr. TILDEN. It ridiculed the Union League and Mr. TILDEN, and exulted in TWEED's triumph over him in 1870; but, in 1871, it said "There were a few indignant protests against the scheme uttered by such high-toned Democrats as Samuel J. Tilden, but they were without *effect*, for Tweed and Sweeny had the voters already bought up."

Finally, these extracts prove not only that Mr. Tilden's narration of the "conspiracy" against the City by the Charter of 1870, and the action under it and the means and objects for which it was obtained, is correct; but that the *Times* knew all about the facts at the time, and that, with that knowledge, it joined the conspiracy and did its utmost to give success to the conspiracy.

The part it took in that transaction was a calamitous mistake, as well as a great wrong to the people.

It might pass silently from the public memory, if the *Times* had not revived the discussion of these events by an effort to apply whatever of credit it gained in 1871 for aiding to undo its 'own work of 1870, to the consummation of a still greater crime in 1873—the creation of a new "Ring," on the ruins of the Municipal Reform Movement, by a new Charter which imitates the fraudulent devices of the Tweed Charter of 1870; and for the purpose of serving that end, had not employed the elaborate and numerous false statements which have made an answer necessary.

www.ingramcontent.com/pod-product-compliance
Lightning Source LLC
Chambersburg PA
CBHW031606110426
42742CB00037B/1312